OSTARA

Llewellyn's Sabbat Essentials

OSTARA

Rituals, Recipes & Lore for the Spring Equinox

Llewellyn Publications
Woodbury, Minnesota

FIRST EDITION
Tenth Printing, 2021

Book design by Donna Burch-Brown
Cover art: iStockphoto.com/16602160/©artcyclone, iStockphoto.
com/24327316/©Allevinatis, iStockphoto.com/18232461/
© Electric_Crayon, iStockphoto.com/4283355/©appleuzr,
Shutterstock/18292789/©NuConcept
Cover design by Kevin R. Brown
Interior illustrations: Mickie Mueller

Llewellyn Publications is a registered trademark of Llewellyn Worldwide Ltd.

Library of Congress Cataloging-in-Publication Data
Connor, Kerri, 1970–
  Ostara : rituals, recipes, and lore for the spring equinox / by Kerri Connor.
— First edition.
     pages cm. ,— (Llewellyn's sabbat essentials ; #1)
  Includes bibliographical references and index.
  ISBN 978-0-7387-4181-9
1. Ostara. I. Title.
  BF1572.O88 C66 2015
  299'.94—dc23   2014021889

Llewellyn Worldwide Ltd. does not participate in, endorse, or have any authority or responsibility concerning private business transactions between our authors and the public.

All mail addressed to the author is forwarded but the publisher cannot, unless specifically instructed by the author, give out an address or phone number.

Any Internet references contained in this work are current at publication time, but the publisher cannot guarantee that a specific location will continue to be maintained. Please refer to the publisher's website for links to authors' websites and other sources.

Llewellyn Publications
A Division of Llewellyn Worldwide Ltd.
2143 Wooddale Drive
Woodbury, MN 55125-2989
www.llewellyn.com

Printed in the United States of America

Contents

beginnings, virtue, renewal, rejuvenation, balance, fertility, change

strength, vernal equinox, sun enters Aries, Libra in the Sou

Green Man, Amalthea, Aphrodite, Blodeuwedd, Eostre, Ea

Flora, Freya, Gaia, Guinevere, Persephone, Libera, M

piter, Umaj, Vela, Aengus MacOg, Cernunnos, Herma, The

ma, Mabon Osiris, Pan, Thor, abundance, growth, health, ca

l healing, patience understanding virtue, spring, honor, contentme

hic abilities, spiritual truth, intuition, receptivity, love, inner sel

rovement, spiritual awareness, purification, childhood, innocence,

ty, creativity, communication, concentration, divination, harmon

bilities, prosperity, attraction, blessings, happiness, luck, money

, guidance, visions, insight, family, wishes, celebrating life cyc

ndship, courage, attracts love, honesty, good health, emotions,

improvement, influence, motivation, peace, rebirth, self preservat

mine power, freedom, optimism, new beginnings, vernal equinox

reation, sun, apple blossom, columbine, crocus, daffodil, daisy,

y, honeysuckle, jasmine, jonquil, lilac, narcissus, orange blossom,

rose, rose, the fool, the magician, the priestess, justice, the star

, gathering, growth, abundance, eggs, seeds, honey, dill, aspara

LLEWELLYN'S SABBAT ESSENTIALS

LLEWELLYN'S SABBAT ESSENTIALS provides instruction and inspiration for honoring each of the modern witch's sabbats. Packed with spells, rituals, meditations, history, lore, invocations, divination, recipes, crafts, and more, each book in this eight-volume series explores both the old and new ways of celebrating the seasonal rites that act as cornerstones in the witch's year.

There are eight sabbats, or holidays, celebrated by Wiccans and many other Neopagans (modern Pagans) today. Together, these eight sacred days make up what's known as the Wheel of the Year, or the sabbat cycle, with each sabbat corresponding to an important turning point in nature's annual journey through the seasons.

Devoting our attention to the Wheel of the Year allows us to better attune ourselves to the energetic cycles of nature and listen to what each season is whispering (or shouting!) to us, rather than working against the natural tides. What better time to start new projects than as the earth reawakens after a long winter, and suddenly everything is blooming and growing and shooting up out of the ground again? And what better time to meditate and plan ahead than during the introspective slumber of winter? With Llewellyn's Sabbat Essentials, you'll learn how to focus on the spiritual aspects of the Wheel of the Year, how to move through it and with it in harmony, and how to celebrate your own ongoing growth and achievements. This may be your first book on Wicca, Witchcraft, or Paganism, or your newest addition to a bookcase or e-reader already crammed with magickal wisdom. In either case, we hope you will find something of value here to take with you on your journey.

Take a Trip Through the Wheel of the Year

The eight sabbats each mark an important point in nature's annual cycles. They are depicted as eight evenly spaced spokes on a wheel representing the year as a whole; the dates on which they fall are nearly evenly spaced on the calendar, as well.

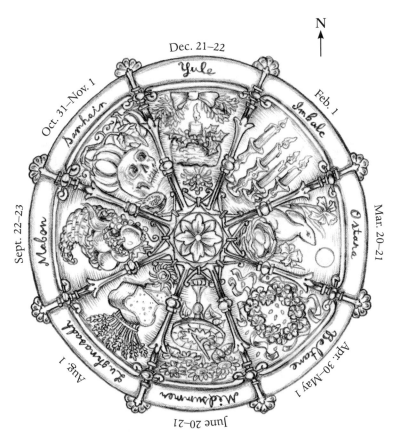

N

Dec. 21–22

Yule

Feb. 1

Imbolc

Oct. 31–Nov. 1

Samhain

Mar. 20–21

Ostara

Sept. 22–23

Mabon

Apr. 30–May 1

Beltane

Aug. 1

Lughnasadh

Midsummer

June 20–21

Wheel of the Year—Northern Hemisphere
(All solstice and equinox dates are approximate,
and one should consult an almanac or a calendar
to find the correct dates each year.)

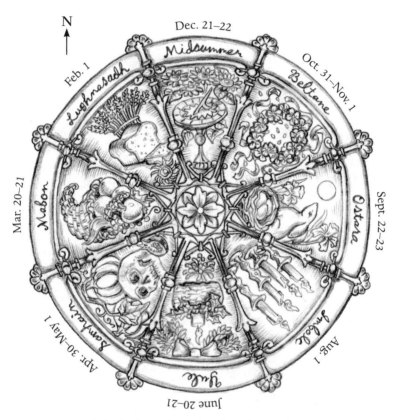

Wheel of the Year—Southern Hemisphere

The wheel is comprised of two groups of four holidays each. There are four solar festivals relating to the sun's position in the sky, dividing the year into quarters: the Spring Equinox, the Summer Solstice, the Fall Equinox, and the Winter Solstice, all of which are dated astronomically and thus vary slightly from year to year. Falling in between these quarter days are the cross-quarter holidays, or fire festivals: Imbolc, Beltane, Lughnasadh, and Samhain. The quarters are sometimes called the Lesser Sabbats and the cross-quarters the Greater Sabbats, although neither cycle is "superior" to the other. In the Southern Hemisphere, seasons are opposite those in the north, and the sabbats are consequently celebrated at different times.

While the book you are holding only focuses on Ostara, it can be helpful to know how it fits in with the cycle as a whole.

The Winter Solstice, also called Yule or Midwinter, occurs when nighttime has reached its maximum length; after the solstice, the length of the days will begin to increase. Though the cold darkness is upon us, there is a promise of brighter days to come. In Wiccan lore, this is the time when the young solar god is born. In some Neopagan traditions, this is when the Holly King is destined to lose the battle to his lighter aspect the Oak King. Candles are lit, feasts are enjoyed, and evergreen foliage is brought in the house as a reminder that, despite the harshness of winter, light and life have endured.

At Imbolc (also spelled Imbolg), the ground is just starting to thaw, signaling that it's time to start preparing the fields for the approaching sowing season. We begin to awaken from our months of introspection and start to sort out what we have learned over that time, while also taking the first steps to make plans for our future. Some Wiccans also bless candles at Imbolc, another symbolic way of coaxing along the now perceptibly stronger light.

On the Spring Equinox, also known as Ostara, night and day are again equal in length, and following this, the days will grow longer than the nights. The Spring Equinox is a time of renewal, a time to plant seeds as the earth once again comes to life. We decorate eggs as a symbol of hope, life, and fertility, and we perform rituals to energize ourselves so that we can find the power and passion to live and grow.

In agricultural societies, Beltane marked the start of the summer season. Livestock were led out to graze in abundant pastures and trees burst into beautiful and fragrant blossom. Rituals were performed to protect crops, livestock, and people. Fires were lit and offerings were made in the hopes of gaining divine protection. In Wiccan mythos, the young god impregnates the young goddess. We all have something we want to harvest by the end of the year—plans we are determined to realize—and Beltane is a great time to enthusiastically get that process in full swing.

The Summer Solstice is the longest day of the year. It's also called Litha, or Midsummer. Solar energies are at their apex, and the power of nature is at its height. In Wiccan lore, it's the time when the solar god's power is at its greatest (so, paradoxically, his power must now start to decrease), having impregnated the maiden goddess, who then transforms into the earth mother. In some Neopagan traditions, this is when the Holly King once again battles his lighter aspect, this time vanquishing the Oak King. It's generally a time of great merriment and celebration.

At Lughnasadh, the major harvest of the summer has ripened. Celebrations are held, games are played, gratitude is expressed, and feasts are enjoyed. Also known as Lammas, this is the time we celebrate the first harvest—whether that means the first of our garden crops or the first of our plans that have come to fruition. To celebrate the grain harvest, bread is often baked on this day.

The Autumn Equinox, also called Mabon, marks another important seasonal change and a second harvest. The sun shines equally on both hemispheres, and the lengths of night and day are equal. After this point, the nights will again be longer than the days. In connection with the harvest, the day is celebrated as a festival of sacrifice and of the dying god, and tribute is paid to the sun and the fertile earth.

To the Celtic people, Samhain marked the start of the winter season. It was the time when the livestock was slaughtered and the final harvest was gathered before the inevitable plunge into the depths of winter's darkness. Fires were lit to help wandering spirits on their way, and offerings were given in the names of the gods and the ancestors. Seen as a beginning, Samhain is now often called the Witches' New Year. We honor our ancestors, wind down our activities, and get ready for the months of introspection ahead … and the cycle continues.

The Modern Pagan's Relationship to the Wheel

Modern Pagans take inspiration from many pre-Christian spiritual traditions, exemplified by the Wheel of the Year. The cycle of eight festivals we recognize throughout modern Pagandom today was never celebrated in full by any one particular pre-Christian culture. In the 1940s and 1950s, a British man named Gerald Gardner created the new religion of Wicca by drawing on a variety of cultures and traditions, deriving and adapting practices from pre-Christian religion, animistic beliefs, folk magick, and various shamanic disciplines and esoteric orders. He combined multicultural equinox and solstice traditions with Celtic feast days and early European agricultural and pastoral celebrations to create a single model that became the framework for the Wiccan ritual year.

This Wiccan ritual year is popularly followed by Wiccans and witches, as well as many eclectic Pagans of various stripes. Some Pagans only observe half of the sabbats, either the quarters or the cross-quarters. Other Pagans reject the Wheel of the Year altogether and follow a festival calendar based on the culture of whatever specific path they follow rather than a nature-based agrarian cycle. We all have such unique paths in Paganism that it is important not to make any assumptions about another's based on your own; maintaining an open and positive attitude is what makes the Pagan community thrive.

Many Pagans localize the Wheel of the Year to their own environment. Wicca has grown to become a truly global religion, but few of us live in a climate mirroring Wicca's British Isles origins. While traditionally Imbolc is the beginning of the thaw and the awakening of the earth, it is the height of winter in many northern climes. While Lammas may be a grateful celebration of the harvest for some, in areas prone to drought and forest fires it is a dangerous and uncertain time of year.

There are also the two hemispheres to consider. While it's winter in the Northern Hemisphere, it's summer in the Southern Hemisphere. While Pagans in America are celebrating Yule and the Winter Solstice, Pagans in Australia are celebrating Midsummer. The practitioner's own lived experiences are more important than any dogma written in a book when it comes to observing the sabbats.

In that spirit, you may wish to delay or move up celebrations so that the seasonal correspondences better fit your own locale, or you may emphasize different themes for each sabbat as you experience it. This series should make such options easily accessible to you.

No matter what kind of place you live on the globe, be it urban, rural, or suburban, you can adapt sabbat traditions and practices to suit your own life and environment. Nature is all around us; no matter how hard we humans try to insulate ourselves from nature's cycles, these recurring seasonal changes are inescapable. Instead of swimming against the tide, many modern Pagans embrace each season's unique energies, whether dark, light, or in between, and integrate these energies into aspects of our own everyday lives.

Llewellyn's Sabbat Essentials series offers all the information you need in order to do just that. Each book will resemble the one you hold in your hands. The first chapter, *Old Ways*, shares the history and lore that have been passed down, from mythology and pre-Christian traditions to any vestiges still seen in modern life. *New Ways* then spins those themes and elements into the manners in which modern Pagans observe and celebrate the sabbat. The next chapter focuses on *Spells and Divination* appropriate to the season or based in folklore, while the following one, *Recipes and Crafts*, offers ideas for decorating your home, hands-on crafts, and recipes that take advantage of seasonal offerings. The chapter *Prayers and Invocations* provides ready-made calls and prayers you may use in ritual, meditation, or journaling. The *Rituals of Celebration* chapter provides three complete rituals: one for a solitary, one for two people, and one for a whole group such as a coven, circle, or grove. (Feel free to adapt each or any ritual to your own needs, substituting your own offerings, calls, invocations, magickal workings, and so on. When planning a group ritual, try to be conscious of any special needs participants may have. There are many wonderful books available that delve into the fine points of facilitating ritual if you don't have experience in this department.) Finally, in the back of the book you'll find a complete list of correspondences for the holiday, from magickal themes to deities to foods, colors, symbols, and more.

By the end of this book you'll have the knowledge and the inspiration to celebrate the sabbat with gusto. By honoring the Wheel of the Year, we reaffirm our connection to nature so that as her endless cycles turn, we're able to go with the flow and enjoy the ride.

OLD WAYS

beginnings, birth, renewal, rejuvenation, balance, fertility, chang

strength, vernal equinox, sun enters Aries, Libra in the Sou

Green Man, Amalthea, Aphrodite, Blodeuwedd, Eostre, E

Flora, Freya, Gaia, Guinevere, Persephone, Libera, A

Enpet, Umaj, Vila, Aengus MacOg, Cernunnos, Herma, The

Kama, Mabon Osiris, Pan, Thor, abundance, growth, health, c

al healing, patience understanding virtue, spring, honor, contentm

psychic abilities, spiritual truth, intuition, receptivity, love, inner se

provement, spiritual awareness, purification, childhood, innocence

ty, creativity, communication, concentration, divination, harmo

abilities, prosperity, attraction, blessings, happiness, luck, money

ty, guidance, visions, insight, family, wishes, celebrating life cy

iendship, courage, attracts love, honesty, good health, emotions

improvement, influence, motivation, peace, rebirth, self preserva

minine power, freedom, optimism, new beginnings, vernal equinox

creation, sun, apple blossom, columbine, crocus, daffodil, daisy

sy, honeysuckle, jasmine, jonquil, lilac, narcissus, orange blosson

nrose, rose, the fool, the magician, the priestess, justice, the sta

s, gathering, growth, abundance, eggs, seeds, honey, dill, expan

*T*HE END OF WINTER is finally at hand. Many people are coming out of a time filled with cold and often darkness as well. For many, the winter months can be downright depressing between a lack of sunshine and bad weather. With the coming of Ostara and spring, the sun is shining once more. The weather is improving and growing warmer each and every day. Birds are returning, flowers are poking through any leftover snow, and grass is turning from a faded yellow-brown back to a vibrant green. While thoughts and projects have been internalized during the winter months, it's now time to focus once again on the world blossoming outside of us.

Ostara, which is also known as the Vernal Equinox, falls generally on March 20 in the Northern Hemisphere (September in the Southern Hemisphere), and marks when the sun hits its zenith, the point on the celestial sphere directly over the equator. Each year the time of the equinox shifts about six hours, making it possible for the precise equinox to fall between March 20 and March 21. Ostara is the official start of spring in the Northern Hemisphere whether you live in an area that is warm year-round, or in an area where the ground is still covered in snow when this date rolls along.

While there is a rather complicated mathematical formula to figure out when the precise equinox will occur, most people are happy to use an almanac, check a calendar, or look up the day or even the precise moment somewhere online.

Though the equinox is said to be equal amounts of day and night (and literally breaks down to mean *equal night*—Latin *aequus* meaning "equal" and *nox* meaning "night"), this isn't exactly true. It all depends on where you live. Those living closer to the equator still see more daylight than darkness, while those farther away from the equator will see less daylight, something that is often overlooked when people talk about us having an equal amount of daylight and nighttime. The most important aspect therefore of the equinox isn't really the amount of daylight or nighttime, it's that moment when the sun does actually hit its zenith. This is something that happens all over the world at the same time. When the sun hits its zenith, it hits it. There is one precise moment in time on that given day when the sun is perfectly lined up with the equator, whether you are in America or Australia. This moment is when spring hits and when light and day begin their triumph over dark and night.

After Yule, because of the tilt of Earth's axis, the sun's light moves farther north and gives those of us in the Northern Hemisphere days that are growing in length. At Ostara, the day and night are close to equal with the sun still growing stronger and the days longer. With more sunlight and the heat given off due to the angle of the sun's rays, the earth begins waking up. From the plants starting to sprout from the ground to the trees growing buds for leaves and flowers to burst from, the animals that come out of hibernation, and others that begin their mating season. It's the time of rebirth and renewal. The cycle of life is starting anew.

Ostara isn't just about chicks and bunnies, nor is it even really about the Goddess Eostre, who gives her name to this festival. While Eostre is said to be a goddess of spring, fertility, and the dawn, there is truly very little information about her. Research shows the first mention of the Goddess Eostre was in the eighth century by a Northumbrian monk named Bede in his 725 CE work titled *De temporum ratione (A Reckoning of Time)*. (Hutton, 180–181) According to Bede, during *Ēosturmōnaþ (the equivalent of April), the Pagans celebrated Eostre with feasts before the Christian holiday Easter came into existence.* The Christian holiday of Easter is named either after Eostre or *Ēosturmōnaþ*, which in turn is thought to be the Proto-Indo-European root for "to shine" or "dawn."

Ronald Hutton tells us in *Stations of the Sun: A History of the Ritual Year in Britain*:

> It falls into that category of interpretations that Bede admitted to be his own, rather than generally agreed or

proven fact. A number of German scholars cast doubt upon its utility during the nineteenth and early twentieth centuries, although not with sufficient evidence to disprove it in turn. Two facts do seem to emerge from the discussion. One is that versions of the name given by Bede were used widely among speakers of Germanic languages during or shortly after his time; thus the Christian festival was known as *Ostarstuopha* in the Main valley during the eighth and ninth centuries. The other is that the Anglo-Saxon *eastre,* signifying both the festival and the season of spring is associated with a set of words in various Indo-European languages, signifying dawn and also goddesses who personified that event, such as the Greek Eos, the Roman Aurora, and the Indian Ushas. (180)

But why isn't there any other information about this goddess before this date? While some scholars agree with this account, others do not. Some claim Eostre to be a Celtic goddess, others a Germanic one, but it's still up for debate whether or not this goddess ever existed or if she was revered and celebrated in the ways we have recently been told. We really don't know much about how she was celebrated other than the description of "feasts," or if she even truly existed at all. While most gods and goddesses have many myths and stories surrounding them, this can't be said for Eostre.

One modern story is found regarding Eostre (other than the claim Easter is named after her). In the story of Eostre, we are told that one day in the winter she found a poor, helpless injured bird that was dying. In order to save the bird's life she turned the bird into a hare, but the change didn't fully take place. While the bird now looked like a hare, it still had the ability to lay eggs. The hare decorated the eggs and then gave them to Eostre as gifts for saving her life. But where did this story come from?

This story is actually based on an Ukranian folk tale that explains the origin of *pysanky*—the beautifully decorated eggs. Eric A. Kimmel retold this tale under the title *The Birds' Gift*. The version including Eostre was first published by Sarah Ban Breathnach in *Mrs. Sharp's Traditions*. From there the story spread, partially through the Internet, until it ended up in the children's magazine *Cricket* under the title "The Coming of Eostre." (Dickman, 16)

Author Adrian Bott gives us this timeline of the connection of Eostre with hares and shows us how what many people believe to be a "tradition" was actually born:

725 CE: Bede mentions Eostre. He does not associate her with hares.

1835: Grimm, in *Deustche Mythologie*, postulates Ostara; he does not associate Eostre with hares.

1874: Adolf Holtzmann states "probably the hare was the sacred animal of Ostara."

1883: K. A. Oberle also states "probably the hare was the sacred animal of Ostara."

1890: Charles Isaac Elton states that Easter customs at "Hare-pie Bank" at "Harecrop Leys" "were probably connected with the worship of the Anglian goddess Eostre."

1892: Charles J. Billson refers to Oberle's association of the hare with Ostara as a conclusion, rather than as a speculation.

1944: John Lanyard states that "the Saxon Easter Goddess does seem to have been connected with the hare."

1976: Christina Hole states that "The hare was the sacred beast of Eastre (or Eostre) a Saxon goddess of Spring and of the dawn." (Bott)

It was Gerald Gardner, while creating Wicca, who pulled together customs from different traditions and came up with seven sabbats and then added in the Vernal Equinox, bringing the total sabbats to eight and putting them approximately six weeks apart.

According to HecatesCauldron.org:

One must realize that nowhere in recorded history did
any one group of pagans practice the entire 8 Sabbats.
Also, there is no record of pagans celebrating the Spring
Equinox. In fact, the Spring Equinox which Gardner calls
Ostara is the Germanic name for their spring Goddess.
Ostara was celebrated in the fourth month of the year,
meaning April, according to the British scribe Bede the
Venerable, writing in the seventh century CE. Over a
thousand years later, she was still honored in Germanic
lands, where her name was used for the month in which
she ruled, April. She did not represent March with its
Spring Equinox.

The fact that people tend to believe that Ostara is an ancient
holiday with an ancient goddess at its core, may not be the
truth, but it has somehow become thought of as law in very
recent history.

Philip Shaw tells us in *Pagan Goddesses in the Early Germanic
World*:

The interpretation of Eostre as a spring goddess has
been strangely influential, given the lack of really clear
evidence to support it. Both skeptics and believers often
refer to her as a spring goddess, and this leads to some

preposterous situations, as when Knobloch (1959: 31–4) argues against the existence of Eostre on the grounds that there is a lack of strong etymological evidence for her connection with the spring. This is clearly no argument against the goddess at all—Knobloch ably demonstrates the weakness of the supposed connection with spring, but this connection is, after all, only one scholarly interpretation of Eostre's name. (55)

While we still don't have any hard evidence of the existence of the goddess Eostre, it doesn't mean you can't celebrate her as a symbol of spring anyway, if that is what you so desire. What she stands for is valid whether her existence can be historically authenticated or not.

Sacred Sites Marking the Equinox

It is believed the ancient Irish people (predating Celts and Druids) celebrated the solstices and the equinoxes. A large part of this proof comes from megalithic cairns built throughout Ireland. While many people believe the Druids built these cairns and henges, scientific testing and dating methods show these monuments and sites to be much older. While the Druids may have eventually used the sites for ritualistic or other practices, they were not responsible for their existence. A particular group of cairns located in Loughcrew contains a passage tomb that is constructed so that a backstone is lit up by the sun's rays on the Vernal Equinox. The backstone contains astronomical symbols that are fully lit at the equinox. (Megalithic Ireland) While this may have been just some sort of elaborate calendar system, the astronomical symbols imply that it did indeed have a greater importance than just marking one day of the year.

The Mayans have celebrated the Spring Equinox for more than 1,000 years. When the sun sets on the ceremonial pyramid El Castillo in Mexico, it creates an illusion known as the "Return of the Sun Serpent." The sun creates what looks to be a giant snake descending the stairs of the pyramid. In this way, they honor the return of their sun god. (Atlas Obscura)

In Vermont, a stone structure incorporated with an amphitheater-type basin, now called "Calendar One," has stones marking where the sun rises on the Summer Solstice and the Vernal and Autumnal Equinoxes. While it is not known for sure what peoples actually built Calendar One, theories abound attributing it to Native Americans even though some of the writings found were actually Irish Hinge Ogham. (Angel) Could the Celts have traveled to North America at some point—even before the current era?

In Salem, New Hampshire, the 4,000-year-old "America's Stonehenge" stands on Mystery Hill. It is believed to have been built by some unknown European migrants or Native Americans. It has five standing stones and one stone that points to the sunrise and sunset at both equinoxes, along with being an accurate astronomical calendar for other events. Several different ancient languages have been discovered at the site, suggesting it was at least used or visited by several different groups of people over its existence. (Goudsward)

Fajada Butte in Chaco Culture National Historical Park, in northwest New Mexico uses stone slabs that cast shadows onto spiral petroglyphs on the cliff wall at the solstices and the equinoxes. Standing at 95 meters high with a 230-meter-long ramp, and no other clear purpose, it is thought this site held extreme ceremonial significance for the Chacoan people. (Sofaer and Sinclair)

Angkor Wat in Cambodia was originally built as a Hindu temple complex in the early twelfth century. On the morning of the Spring Equinox, the sun climbs the side of the central tower where it will rest briefly at the very top of the temple spire. (Van de Bogart)

Mnajdra in Malta dates back approximately 5,000 years. It is thought to be one of the world's oldest solar calendars, marking the solstices and the equinoxes. On the Spring Equinox, the sun's rays enter the temple and illuminate the main axis. (Heritage Malta)

Fernacre Stone Circle in Cornwall is situated on a slope surrounded by hills that directly mark three of the cardinal directions: Brown Willy stands due east, Rough Tor is due north, and Garrow Tor lies south. At sunrise on the morning of the equinox, Brown Willy marks the point of the sunrise. (Cornwall's Archaeological Heritage)

In 2009, the 12,000-year-old Spout Run Paleoindian site was discovered in Clarke County, Virginia. The Department of Historic Resources added the site to the Virginia Landmarks Register in 2011, showing that ancient sites are still being discovered even today. At this site, both concentric rings and a triangular rock formation have been shown to align with the equinox. After discovering incised markings, archaeologist Jack Hranicky said, "It appears the incising is the shape of two foot prints. When stood on, during the Equinox, the sun causes a halo effect over the person standing on the prints." (White)

All of these sites, and many more, mark the position of the sun on the day of the equinox. Whether these sites were created as spiritual places for ritualistic events or simply to mark the passage of time as a calendar, we may never know for sure. However, we have seen over time, groups all over the world have celebrated and honored the astronomical occurrences they saw in the skies above them. Even though it was Gerald Gardner who turned the Vernal Equinox into what we now know as modern-day Ostara, it is clear that for thousands of years, not only did people know that the equinox existed and occurred, they kept track of when it would happen as it must have held some sort of significance for them. Whether they saw it as a time of balance, a time of new beginnings, or simply as a time to plant, people took notice of the equinox and marked its occurrence often in elaborate ways with grandiose, complicated structures.

Ostara's Relationship to Other Holidays

The themes of Ostara are most closely associated with the Christian Easter, though they don't always fall very close on the calendar. Easter is held on the first Sunday after the first full moon that happens either on or after the Vernal Equinox, unless that full moon is itself on a Sunday, then Easter is delayed a week. Debates still go on as to whether or not Easter was "stolen" from Ostara (or any pre-Christian equinox feasts of fertility) or the other way around.

At Easter, Christians celebrate the resurrection of Jesus Christ, considered to be the son of God, who was sacrificed two days earlier on Good Friday. This provides a parallel with the themes of resurrection and rebirth often shared with Ostara. Although Jesus himself is not "reborn," he was resurrected from his tomb, and because he had died for the sins of those who believe in him, those people have the chance to be "reborn" through him. Modern Easter, like Ostara, is celebrated with springtime imagery of eggs, baby chicks, and bunnies, emphasizing new life rather than the tomb of death. The Christian symbolism of the lamb is due to the fact that Jesus's death during Passover made him a "Passover lamb."

The Jewish holiday of Passover (the fifteenth day of Nisan, which begins on the night of the full moon after the northern Vernal Equinox), is a very somber holiday that celebrates the exodus of the Israelites out of Egypt. Before the Pharaoh let the Israeli slaves go, God inflicted ten plagues upon the Egyptians, the last one being the death of each first born into an Egyptian home. In order to save their children, the Jews were instructed to paint their doorways with the blood of a lamb so the spirit of God knew to pass over and leave the inhabitants unharmed.

But there have always been many other holidays and deities associated with this time of year besides Passover and Easter. While the Druids didn't celebrate Ostara, they did have their own holiday known as Alban Eiler, which translates into "Light of the Earth." It was the day that both the night and the day stood as equals. This was the day that crops were to be sown, and it was seen as a time of transition. Many believe the Druids thought this to be a highly magickal time. (The Sacred Fire)

Bacchanalia was a festival held in March to celebrate the wine Gods Bacchus and Dionysus. This festival had very little to do with the celebration of the equinox other than the timing; its celebration wasn't about the day and night being equal but about wine and physical pleasure. These parties were often described as wild and excessive orgies where even violence and murder took place in the chaos. (Gill) In comparison, Gardner's idea of Ostara is somewhat of a peaceful gift that instead celebrates rebirth, renewal, and revitalization. Modern Pagans are more apt to binge on chocolate eggs than wine at this holiday.

The Celebration of Springtime Deities

When working with deities at this time of year, we are best suited by choosing ones that embody the spirit of life and renewal. Traditionally at this time of year, maiden goddesses have reigned and been honored, while the attention of the gods goes to the young virile male gods. Those associated with the spring, animals, rebirth, and hunting have been celebrated the most.

In Ancient Greece, Dionysus and Persephone were both celebrated as the deities of spring. Dionysus, a god of plants, grape vines especially, was said to be in terrible pain throughout the winter months. In spring his strength would return with the flowering of the earth. (Ireland's Druidschool)

Persephone, the daughter of Demeter who was goddess of the crops and harvest, was kidnapped by Hades. Demeter was so upset over her missing daughter, she was unable to tend to the crops, which began to die off. Zeus sent Hermes to speak with Hades about releasing Persephone so that the crops would not completely die off and the people would be able to live. Hermes brokered a deal with Hades that allowed Persephone to return to her mother in the spring for six months.

After her time was up, she would return to the underworld to live as Hades's queen each year. Demeter, delighting in the return of her daughter, ensures that each spring the flowers are blooming in order to greet Persephone on her return.

Aphrodite, the Greek goddess of beauty, love, pleasure, and procreation, was said to have flowers spring up at her feet as she walked on the land when first rising from the foam of the sea. She is connected to the generative powers of nature and therefore is highly connected to the spring as the earth comes back to life. Some considered her the mother of all living things and each spring she births the world into life again.

Venus, the Roman goddess of love and beauty, is associated with cultivated fields and gardens and is seen as the Roman equivalent of Aphrodite. Her association with the cultivated fields and gardens ties her into the spring theme of new beginnings, whether this is new beginnings relating to the vegetation of the earth or the figurative vegetation of the soul. Two temples dedicated to Venus existed, one in Lavinium and the other at Ardea. (Lindemans)

Perhaps one of the saddest stories of a goddess celebrated in the spring belongs to that of the Greek Clytie. Clytie began her life as a water nymph who was in love with the sun god Apollo. In some versions of the story, her love is unreturned and so she sits forever watching him cross the sky each day. Eventually her legs and feet grow into the soil and turn into roots, her body takes on the form of a stem, her arms turns to leaves, while her face becomes a heliotrope that continues to watch the sun cross the sky each day. In other versions of the story, she is transformed into a flower after having sex with the sun god. (McCoy, 122)

Cybele is a goddess who has been celebrated in many different countries including Phrygia, Greece, and Rome. Her followers were many, as she was one of the most famous creator goddesses. Other than new life, she is associated with the earth, passion, and love, making her a perfect goddess to be celebrated at the beginning of the spring. In Rome, she was known as the Great Mother. (McCoy, 122; Jordan, 169)

The Greek Eos was the goddess of the dawn, which is also associated with spring for its aspect of a new beginning. Eos was also a very sexual goddess, which ties in with the themes of romance, love, and fertility.

The Roman Flora, goddess of flowers, is often celebrated at the equinox and does have her own additional festival day, Floralia, which was held on April 27 (now April 28) (McCoy, 123; Jordan, 96–97) between Ostara and Beltane. As the goddess of flowers, she is another perfect goddess to celebrate at this time of year. If you would prefer to work with a Celtic goddess, Blodeuwedd was magickally made of flowers, making her an ideal goddess to work with at Floralia as well.

The Norse goddess Freya left the earth during the winter and would return to it each spring. (McCoy, 123) Another goddess of sexuality, life, and death, she too fits right in with the themes of the season.

Gaia being one of the oldest Greek goddesses of all, is literally depicted as being the earth. She made all living things and is literally the Earth Mother. When spring rolls along, she awakens and her beautiful transformations take place and her creations come to life.

The Hindu goddess Rati is the consort of Kama, the god of love. Rati herself is the goddess of love, lust, passion, and sexual pleasure. Putting these two together is a wonderful combination to celebrate love and passion at the beginning of spring. (McCoy, 124)

Not to be outdone by the women, there are many gods associated with the spring as well.

The Irish Aengus MacOg was a young god of love and romance. Being the son of the Dagda, he is also a god of regeneration (McCoy, 92; Jordan, 5), an important aspect of spring as this is when things are regenerated, or brought back to life.

The Celtic god Cernunnos, also known as the Horned God, is one of the best known. With his rack of deer antlers spouting from his head, it is clear to see he is a god of the woodlands and nature. He also is the consort of the Earth Mother, whom he mates with in order to give birth to all living things. He is basically the Earth Father.

The Irish "Good God" Dagda is the ultimate god of regeneration. He owns a cauldron that brings dead warriors back to life. He is able to resurrect that which has died.

The Green Man is a great representation of spring. Imagine him coming alive and growing as each tree bud grows a little larger and then bursts into a flower or a leaf. Imagine him romping through the woods encouraging the flowers to break through the ground and bloom. He encourages the vines to grab ahold of trees and climb their way upward toward the sun's light. He is alive in all plant life, encouraging it to grow and thrive.

The Welsh god Mabon may already have a sabbat named after him, but he is also a god who retreats to the underworld during the winter and then returns in the spring. (McCoy, 94) While Mabon is a good time to celebrate the prowess of this god, Ostara is an excellent time to celebrate his return to the world.

The Egyptian god Min, who is depicted with a giant phallus, is obviously a god of fertility and creation. Spring is the perfect time to honor this god of reproduction as the animals and the land itself begin producing and reproducing themselves. (McCoy, 95; Jordan, 199)

Another Egyptian god, Osiris, changes roles throughout the year. In the spring, he is a god of fertility and vegetation, ensuring that the crops are planted and that they thrive. (McCoy, 95;

Jordan, 235–236) Osiris is another god who was resurrected, he by his sister wife, the great goddess Isis.

The Greek god Pan is a god of nature, the woods, and the animals in the woods. When thinking of Pan, think of forests, frolicking, and fun because those are all associated with him. Spring is the time to get out in the woods and experience getting back to nature and celebrating the new life with Pan as your guide.

The Norse god Thor and his magickal hammer Mjölnir were quite handy to have around at the beginning of spring. Thor simply had to smash through the ice with Mjölnir and brush winter away to bring the spring in. (McCoy, 96)

Each of these deities has their own connection with the season of spring and many with either regeneration or simply with the blossoming earth as well. They embody and celebrate the newness of the world around us as we step from the dark half of the year into the light.

New Year, New Life

Up until 1752, when the switch from the Roman Julian Calendar to the Gregorian Calendar occurred, March 25 was considered the beginning of the new year. In England, Lady Day was the celebration of the Virgin Mary, held on March 25. Lady Day was considered the perfect time for the new year to begin based on the ancient traditions of the equinox being the start of a new year. (McCoy, 107–108)

With the equinox being the beginning of the year, this explains why Aries (March 21–April 19) is the first sign of the zodiac year. This also helps to explain the names of some of our months a bit more as well. September (*septem* meaning "seven") seems an odd choice for the ninth month, October (*octo* meaning "eight") for the tenth month, November (*novem* meaning "nine") for the eleventh month, and December (*decem* or *dec* meaning "ten") for the twelfth month. With March being the first month, April would have been second, May was third, June was fourth, July was fifth, August was the sixth month, and then you can see how the rest fall into place and go in the numerical order their name actually means.

Nowruz, which translates into "new day," was the ancient Persian celebration of the new year on the Vernal Equinox up to 3,000 years before the current era. This day was so important that the King of Babylon was only seen as the legitimate king after participating in the Nowruz festival. (Trotter, 108) Zoroastrianism was the religion of ancient Persia before the advent of Islam and this kept Nowruz alive as a holiday. While only celebrated as a holy day for Sufi Muslims, Bektashis, Ismailis, Alawites, Alevis, Babis, and followers of the Bahá'í Faith, others in areas such as Afghanistan, Turkey, and Iran still celebrate it as a secular holiday. In 2010, the General Assembly of the United Nations recognized the International Day of Nowruz, stating it is a spring festival of Persian origin that has been celebrated for centuries. (United Nations)

Ostara also gives us the chance to begin working on our internal selves anew, just like New Year's Day. We till our own internal fields and plant our own emotional, mental, spiritual, or even physical crops that we hope to harvest by the end of the light half of the year so we can use the dark half of the year to rest and to make plans again for the next light half of the year. These plans can be about virtually anything, whether it is learning a new skill, starting a new exercise program, building an addition onto your home, or anything at all. Now is the time to start projects, especially anything that is new to you. It is a time of hope, growth, and anticipation, fitting for the sign of Aries. Anything is possible, and optimism is at an all-time high. Set your goals high; if you don't reach them all this year, you can carry some over to the next year, but be optimistic that you can attain whatever it is you set your heart and mind to.

Chicks, eggs, and bunnies have been thought of as symbols of Ostara because of their connection to rebirth, renewal, and fertility. Rabbits multiply rapidly and in great numbers. Every month a rabbit can give birth since the gestation period runs from twenty-eight to thirty-two days, with litters ranging from six to twelve babies. A chicken can lay an egg just about every day, and though they may not all be fertilized, those that are will become a chick in just twenty-one days. In about six months, the chick is a full-grown hen and will start laying eggs of her own. Even unfertilized eggs have their uses by being consumed and providing nourishment for either humans or other animals.

The phoenix is known to be a magickal creature of optimism. The phoenix, a beautiful bird, lives its life until it perishes in flames but then resurrects itself from its own ashes for a brand-new beginning and starts life anew. It is another ideal representation of Ostara as it ties in with the themes of resurrection, new beginnings, and hope for the future. We all crash and burn sometimes. Perhaps there is something you tried to do in the past but it just didn't work out. It may not have been a total failure after all, it may have been bad timing. Use this time to look through your life at those times when you did crash and burn. Is there a way to resurrect that failure from the ashes and start over again? Perhaps it was a failed relationship that you want to rekindle, or at least end on better terms. Perhaps it was a missed opportunity at a relationship or some other adventure. Perhaps you had taken a class and failed it. Now is the time to go back through those mess-ups and missed opportunities and decide which ones you want to try again and start over with. Resurrect old ideas with a new enthusiasm. Projects or ideas that failed before may be successful this time around by being started at a time designed for hope and new beginnings.

The pooka is another magickal creature associated with this time of year, particularly through the Alban Eiler aspect. A pooka is a mysterious and mischievous shape-shifting Irish creature of the fey. Before the pooka got a bad reputation, he was seen as a servant who helped to bring in the power of the Vernal Equinox to the land, woods, and fields. He may even have been a lover of the Goddess herself. Due to his physical makeup (often seen as half man, half rabbit—though he can be a combination of other creatures as well), he has a strong tie to rabbits, the symbol of fertility and potency.

While the day of the equinox itself is about balance, it's important to remember that balance is fleeting, and the fact of the matter is true balance very seldom exists. Even on the equinox, depending on your location, night and day still are not completely equal. The farther you are from the equator, the bigger the difference between reality and equality. We can work to achieve balance, and work to maintain it, but truly keeping balance stable is a difficult task since life and circumstances are constantly changing. The equinox is also not only about balance. It's the beginning of the triumph of light over dark, warmth over cold, and day over night. It is the beginning of new life.

NEW WAYS

strength, vernal equinox, sun enters Aries, Libra in the Sco...
Green Man, Amalthea, Aphrodite, Blodeuwedd, Eostre, E...
...Flora, Freya, Gaia, Guinevere, Persephone, Libera, ...
...npet, Umaj, Vela, Aengus Mac Og, Cernunnos, Herma, The
...ama, Mabon Osiris, Pan, Thor, abundance, growth, health, e...
...al healing, patience understanding virtue, spring, honor, contents
...hic abilities, spiritual truth, intuition, receptivity, love, inner s...
...provement, spiritual awareness, purification, childhood, innocenc...
...ity, creativity, communication, concentration, divination, harmo...
...abilities, prosperity, attraction, blessings, happiness, luck, mone...
...y, guidance, visions, insight, family, wishes, celebrating life cy...
...iendship, courage, attracts love, honesty, good health, emotions,
...improvement, influence, motivation, peace, rebirth, self preserva...
...nine power, freedom, optimism, new beginnings, vernal equino...
...reation, sun, apple blossom, columbine, crocus, daffodil, daisy...
...ry, honeysuckle, jasmine, jonquil, lilac, narcissus, orange blossom...
...nrose, rose, the fool, the magician, the priestess, justice, the sta...
...s, gathering, growth, abundance, eggs, seeds, honey, dill, aspara...

$\mathcal{S}$PRING IS IN the air. Baby animals are romping through the forest and prancing in the meadows. Flowers are bursting through the ground—and in some places even through the snow—and blooming. The trees are forming buds that grow larger every day; some will soon be flowers that will grow into fruits, and other buds will grow into leaves to help collect the nutrients the trees need to grow and thrive. The birds have built nests and eggs will soon be hatching with babies chirping to be fed. For those in the north, the red-breasted robin has returned. New life is being seen all around us, and we all know spring is well on its way.

The grass is once again growing (along with weeds!) and for many people the lawn mowers will be coming out for the first time. For those living in areas where gardens are possible, tilling has begun, and in the south, seeds may already be in the ground. In some parts of the country, March 17 (St. Patrick's Day) is a traditional day to plant peas in order to harvest early June peas.

While the outside world is busy going about numerous changes, many people will notice an inner change going on as well. Perhaps you have been suffering from a slight case, or even a major one, of cabin fever. You may feel overly tired, trapped, or claustrophobic. You may suffer from seasonal affective disorder and literally need the sunshine. You feel the need to get out and enjoy yourself outdoors, even if it is just a quick outing. Maybe a day in the park or even just a walk around the block is just the thing you need to start feeling like your old self again. If it is warm enough, you may want to start yard work, gardening, or something that will help you reconnect with the earth and the enlivening world around you.

It's time to shake off the old and start anew. This is one of the reasons spring cleaning is so popular. Cleaning out the old and making way for the new always helps to give us a renewed sense of purpose. Whether it is a cleaning out of your physical home or your emotional or spiritual home, sometimes old messes need to be cleared out to make way for new and fresh ideas and plans. If you are hung up on an old project that isn't getting you anywhere, it's time to rethink your plans and revamp them if necessary. Moving forward on goals set in motion during the dark half of the year is what this feeling of rebirth and regeneration is all about.

It's time to take something old, fix it up, and make it new again—whether it is a home, an antique dresser, or even yourself. During the dark half of the year, we spent some time taking inventory and making plans, during the light half of the year we turn those plans into actions. For some Pagans this is their version of the more common New Year's resolutions. When the light starts taking control over the darkness once again, we get up, we get out, and we act, turning those thoughts, dreams, and plans into reality.

For other people, the saying "love is in the air" is all too true. Whether it be a romantic, lustful, or even a platonic love, relationships also blossom this time of year. For those who are already involved, it may be time to renew that love as the feelings of friskiness take over the entire animal kingdom. (We are just mammals after all!) There is a reason we feel this way when spring hits us. It's intuition at its finest. With the feelings of newness in the air, we want to rekindle those feelings of when our relationships were new and young and filled with energy, passion, and spark. We either try to recreate or reinvent those feelings. Sometimes when those attempts fail, we move on to create and find those intense feelings in a new place. These attempts sometimes fail, in which case we simply have to remind ourselves of the age old adage, *nothing ventured, nothing gained,* and, like the phoenix, rise from the ashes and start all over again.

Maybe it's simply time for you to find a relationship, whether it is a romantic or a platonic one. After being cooped up for the winter, whether figuratively or literally or both, we long for connections and reconnections with others. It's time to get out and make those connections and build bridges with others. Make an effort to get out and meet people. Find new groups to join to meet people who have similar interests. The time for hiding indoors is over and done, it's time to get out and welcome the world into your life.

For many people, spring brings with it the opportunity to grow in other ways, literally to garden. More and more people are going back to growing their own food, no matter where they live. The ideas of organic and homegrown are on the rise more and more every year. Those who have their own land may put in large crops or a small garden plot. Others who live in the city with smaller yards may only have room for container gardening. Many apartments have small balconies or patios where even more types of food can be grown in containers. Container gardening can also be done inside in front of a large window of an apartment with herbs, lettuce, or other small plants that don't need to have flowers pollinated in order to produce food. It is very important in container gardening to keep giving the soil nutrients, however, as when there is less dirt to get the nutrients from, the plants will quickly go through it. What start off as beautiful, lush green plants will wither and die halfway through the season if they do not have the proper nutrients to keep them going. Recipes for organic plant foods and composting can be found online.

Setting your gardening schedule to the same schedule as other projects in your life can be beneficial. Begin working on projects the same time you plant your physical garden and watch both grow as time goes by.

Even if you can't do any physical gardening, there is plenty of gardening of the mind, body, and spirit to do! Now would be a great time to start a meditation practice if you don't already have one. How about taking up yoga, Pilates, or even belly dance? These are all forms of exercise for the body, soul, and spirit. Maybe you have always wanted to learn how to read tarot cards, practice Reiki, or read auras. Maybe you want to learn how to cleanse your chakras. Whatever you want to do, you can. You only have to step up and start.

Making anything new into a daily practice can be difficult at first. Finding the time and sticking with it are often the two most difficult parts of adding a new element to your life, but even if you start with just fifteen minutes a day, you will soon find yourself making more time to do the things you enjoy doing. If something you try just isn't doing it for you, and after a few weeks you find yourself dreading it or looking at it as a chore, it probably isn't for you. Don't feel bad about giving something up once you have given it a fair chance. Not every practice is for every person, and there is nothing wrong with that. People are born with different talents and interests and they develop different skill sets all the time. This doesn't mean you failed, it simply means you are budgeting and planning your time for what is showing to be successful for you. Just make sure you give it a fair chance. A meditation practice will not have the chance to grow if you only try for two days any more than a seed will have the chance to germinate, grow, and produce food if you only water it for two days.

These are all ways to use the energies at this time of year of renewal and new beginnings for your own benefit or even for the benefit of others.

Seasonal Activities

There are many ways to celebrate the season of Ostara. I say the "season of Ostara" as many people don't spend just one day in celebration. While a ritual may take place on a certain day, that does not necessarily mean that is when the celebration begins and ends.

Taking a spring walk is a great way to welcome the new life and growth in the world and to share in it. Even if the air is still slightly crisp, a walk in the beginning of spring is like no other time. If you live in an area where there is snow, try to get out on a warm day when the sun is out and the snow is melting. Not only are the sights something to see, but the scents of melting snow, the earthy mud breaking through the snow, and maybe even crocuses or other early flowers blooming are something to take in. Also there is something you can only hear when these conditions are just right: the snow actually melting and the water running across the frozen ground or the drips of water from icicles overhead. If you can find a park or a nature preserve that contains a small stream or creek, you can hear this sound even more so as the waters from the melting snow rush down the banks in search of the stream to carry them away.

A walk at this time of year can be more physically challenging than at any other time of year, depending on the conditions. You may be battling snow, mud, and cold, or you may have an absolutely dry and gorgeous day depending on where you live. While some places have very mild weather in the early spring, others are still fighting snow into April. Still, just because a walk may be difficult doesn't mean a person shouldn't give it a try, it simply means you get to start your new year off with a challenge. Just the idea of starting off with a challenge will be a new challenge for some people! For others, challenging themselves is a daily way of life. In this time of renewal, rebirth, and regeneration, why not start off with something new?

Another activity people often take part in at this time of year, especially families, is kite flying. Again this can be a difficult task depending on where you live and what your weather conditions are like, but you do need some wind to get a kite soaring through the air—and staying there—and March is often a very good time for wind! The act of kite flying can truly be a spiritual experience if you make it so. It is a great way to teach children about the element of air, which is also associated with new beginnings, and also about grounding. Kite flying is a really good metaphor for how we can send our energy and intentions out into the universe while staying firmly grounded. It also teaches us that while we may sometimes dream with our head in the clouds, we need to ensure our feet are planted on the earth. When we lose connection with the ground and don't keep track of what our feet are doing, we can end up tripping, heading the wrong direction, or even falling, and then our kite comes crashing out of the sky. This translates to our spiritual life in the same manner. When we don't keep ourselves grounded and balanced, things can come crashing down around us.

In many modern celebrations at Ostara there is a blessing of the seeds; these can be either literal or figurative seeds. If you are a gardener of any sort, bless the seeds at Ostara, especially ones that need to be started early indoors. Depending on where you live, the actual field or garden plot can be blessed at Beltane. If you are in a climate where you can plant before Beltane however, you can go ahead and bless the land now, too. You can also bless any figurative seeds you want to plant and sow this year. This may be done by writing a list of the goals you want to accomplish or your hopes and dreams and then using the list in your ritual. You can also just add some quiet reflection time during your ritual for everyone to think about what seeds he or she want to plant and germinate in their own lives. In a more symbolic way of planting your goals, you can write them out on a piece of paper and actually bury them in a garden plot or even a planter filled with dirt that will eventually contain seeds or a garden plant. This way as the plant grows, your goals do as well.

With the feeling of "newness" in the air, it's fun to be able to do kidlike things again. In the spring we can feel young again. We can act young again. The Goddess is in her maiden form, and the God is a young virile man filled with energy and strength. A perfect way to honor them is to emulate them and take on similar forms and attitudes no matter what our physical age is. You are only as old as you let yourself feel. There are a variety of activities that both adults and kids will be able to enjoy together and it all falls under the heading of PLAY. From finger painting to playing old-fashioned outdoor games, play should always be an important part of our lives, but it's often one we totally forget about. Getting into the habit of playing again is a perfect way to honor the spring.

Outdoor finger painting on a sunny day provides for easy clean up and is another way to teach children about the elements. You can have them paint representations of each element. You can explain that while outside, they are taking in the element of air, and through the paints they are working with the element of water. Finger painting tends to have a calming, grounding effect on the participants, so you can discuss this aspect as well.

Play that involves using our whole bodies is a perfect release in the spring after being cooped up all winter long. It's time to get out and move and get some energy building and circulating through the body once again. What were some of your favorite outdoor games as a kid? Red rover? Freeze tag? Kick the can? Hide and seek? Ghosts in the graveyard? Even duck, duck, goose. Do your kids know how to play these games? It's amazing how many kids these days don't.

Playing with Eggs

Springtime activities are often about getting outside and enjoying the great outdoors, and another way to do that is with a fun little object known as a *cascarone*. A five-second Internet search on cascarones will immediately show you that they originated in China or Italy or Mexico. Most people agree they are a Mexican tradition, but there are those who will insist they started elsewhere. The concept of the cascarone is simple—a blown out egg is refilled with something else. You can order papier-mâché cascarones online or buy them in stores around the equinox with the Easter decorations. You can also make them yourself using regular chicken eggs (look for instructions in the Recipes and Crafts chapter). Prefilled papier-mâché cascarones are generally filled with confetti, though you may be able to find ones with small toys or candy as well.

Cascarones are a great way to bestow blessings on someone. They use the symbol of the fertile egg to "birth" or "hatch" those qualities for the intended.

Dust off the winter cobwebs and plan your Ostara time to include some serious playdate time for yourself and your family. There are so many different activities you can do with eggs. In fact, you could literally do an egg activity a day for weeks and not have to duplicate. There are plenty of egg games and activities far better suited for outdoor fun than indoor fun. Some of these activities include egg rolls and several other types of egg races. In a traditional American-style egg roll, long-handled spoons are used to push a (usually) hard-boiled egg from starting line to finish line. The most famous egg roll in America takes place at Easter at the White House. Similar games are played in other countries. In Germany, a track is built out of sticks for eggs to be rolled down. The fastest egg is the winner. In Denmark, decorated eggs are rolled down a slope or a hill. The egg that travels the farthest distance is the winner. In Lithuania, a game is played similar to marbles—you roll your egg and get to keep any eggs that your egg touches.

The most common of egg races is most likely one where you use a spoon to carry an egg from starting line to finish. Again these are often hard-boiled eggs, but fresh eggs can be used as well. With fresh eggs, you can add in the rule that if the egg breaks you have to start all over with a new egg.

Another type of egg race is having to carry the egg somewhere on your body without using your hands. Again, often done with hard-boiled eggs, but the added risk of mess with a fresh egg can add to the fun. You may have people carry the egg between their thighs, where they have to be careful not to squeeze hard enough to break it, but they do have to squeeze hard enough to not drop it. This can also be done with an egg being held between the chin and neck, or use two eggs—one in each underarm. To make things really difficult and silly (especially if adults are playing), try a round with all four eggs in place at once.

An even more difficult type of race for a large number of people is often played with something larger, such as an orange or a grapefruit. In this team race, everyone keeps their hands behind their back and passes an egg from one person to the next. The catch is you hold the egg between your chin and neck and have to pass it off to the next person for them to hold in between their chin and neck as well. It takes a lot of twisting and contorting to get into the right position to pass the egg without dropping it. The first team to pass the egg through all members wins! This game can also be done with either fresh or hard-boiled eggs, but since it is so difficult to do, you may want to take it easy on your family and friends and give them the hard-boiled option.

Another activity is egg tosses where teams of two toss an egg back and forth getting farther apart each time. The team who is able to get the farthest apart without breaking their egg wins. These games are fun for kids or adults, and they really get your blood pumping and your body moving again.

Egg tapping, or "jarping," is a competition where people tap the pointy end of their hard-boiled egg against other eggs. Once an egg cracks, it is out of the competition and the egg that cracks the most other eggs is the winner. While this game can be played either inside or out, you can change things up a bit by making this an outdoor game that is played with fresh eggs instead of hard-boiled! Yes it may make a bit of a mess, but egg is easily cleaned up with a hose.

The egg dance may actually go back hundreds of years, but for many people this is a little-known tradition that seemed to have been far more popular in Germany and the United Kingdom than it ever was in America. Perhaps it's time to change that and make the egg dance an annual event at your Ostara gathering. The concept is easy. Fill an area (preferably outdoors in the grass) with eggs scattered about and then dance in that same area while trying to avoid destroying the eggs. There are many fun "springy" songs that would go along great with this activity such as "O' She Will Bring" by Alice Di Micele, just about any version of "Lord of the Dance," or Lisa Thiel's "Ostara (Spring Song)."

Get Out and Go Somewhere!

Spring field trips are great because they give you a chance to get out and about and away from the place where you may be feeling like you just spent way too much time over the winter months. If it's a chilly or rainy day, opt for some indoor options including art galleries, museums, aquariums, or a planetarium if you are lucky enough to have one near you. Planetariums will often have special shows or exhibits explaining more about the equinox and how it works.

On warmer, sunnier days, a trip to a local zoo will not only get you outside, it will help you get in touch with a whole different kind of nature than what you are generally used to. Spend some real time exploring the animals. Use all of your senses to get to know these animals better. Watch how they interact with each other and their surroundings. Perhaps they will even interact with you. Listen to the way they communicate. You probably won't have much of an issue smelling some of them, but others may be far more difficult or even impossible to tell what scent they give off. Often the baby animals are brought out in special exhibits with their mother at zoos during the spring as well. While some people are terribly against the idea of zoos and keeping these animals in captivity, some zoos specialize and only house special-needs animals that would not be able to survive very long in their own natural habitat. These zoos often have some type of animal adoption program where you can donate money to the care of a certain animal or a species of animal. Perhaps this is a way for you to help give new life to something else and pay it forward.

Some people might not have a zoo close by but instead might have some type of farm attraction you can go to. Even domesticated farm animals are a type of nature and a way to get in touch with your animal side. Perhaps you live near a more exotic kind of farm. For example, an ostrich, llama, or alpaca ranch may be local to you and open to the public. Each of these places will give you a different experience and most likely teach you something entirely new.

Spring is the time when the farmers' markets start to open. Your location will dictate what is available at your own local market. Many start the spring with very few vegetables, but other products such as eggs, meats, cheese, and wine are often available. Farmers' markets can also be very educational—from information received to other activities such as demonstrations that may be scheduled to go on during the day.

Even if the weather isn't perfect, you can still get outside. When was the last time you played in the rain? Grab some rain boots, a poncho, and an umbrella if you must, but get outside and enjoy the element of water as it falls down all around you. Instead of avoiding those puddles on the ground, take a great big leap and jump right into the middle of it instead. Splash the people around you (as long as they are people you know and not complete strangers—they might not take too kindly to it!).

Pull a Gene Kelly and dance and sing in the rain. You don't even have to be good at dancing or singing, just do it! Let yourself be free enough to enjoy yourself and to enjoy the water as it washes down over you. Remember, water washes away the old, the dirt, and the grime, making way for a clean new start. Water is also essential to the survival of all living things. While we need to take in water to survive, we may find that playing in it also is vital to our very existence. In this time of renewal and rejuvenation, let nature take its course and do its job, washing away what you need gone so you can start anew and refreshed. If you're brave enough, try singing and dancing in public in the rain. You may be surprised to see how contagious this simple little act can be.

While all of these activities are ideal ways to get yourself moving this spring, they really can be done at any time. The themes associated with each, however, make them ideal (particularly if you are a parent raising your child in a Pagan setting) for the rebirth of nature and the earth that takes place at Ostara.

Pagan Ways of Celebrating Ostara

For the day of Ostara itself, you will probably want to include some type of ritual. As stated before, during a ritual is a good time to bless the seeds you want to sow and plant throughout the year—both literal food and/or flower seeds and figuratively speaking mental, spiritual, or even physical seeds. But there are other aspects to your ritual or celebration you may want to include as well.

Meditations can always be included in a ritual or performed before or after the ritual. There are many different guided meditations you can work with, or you may create your own or have a silent meditation on a chosen subject. Some meditations will also be provided for you later on in this book.

Many of those who do celebrate Ostara still honor the goddess Eostre. Her symbols include rabbits, eggs, and chicks, along with other baby animals. These symbols are representative of fertility and not just the fertility of the land and the animals, but the fertility of the mind as well.

Pastel colors are often used at Ostara as they are the colors we see in the natural world around us as the vegetation starts growing again and blooms. New grass is a light color—not the dark green we get after several rains and long days of sun. The flowers that burst through the snow first are usually white or have a lighter shade. You won't see deep red roses blooming on Ostara, but you may find crocuses and daffodils. These are the most common decorations for Ostara by far. This celebration tends to focus more on the coming of spring, the awakening of the earth, and the rebirth of new projects or ideas.

With the symbol of eggs being so popular, now is the time for egg hunts—whether these be real, colored eggs or plastic eggs filled with candy, money, and/or small toys. Egg hunts don't have to be just for kids. Adults can join in on the fun with eggs designed especially for them. Plastic eggs can be filled with small pieces of paper that contain quotes, affirmations, or specific blessings such as "May the finder of this egg be blessed with prosperity."

Coloring eggs is another fun activity. There are literally dozens of commercial egg-coloring kits on the market these days, from specific cartoon characters to glittery eggs to metallics and pastels. Kids can now color eggs in a multitude of colors and styles. You may want to try a more traditional approach and use foods and plants to make your own natural colorings. You can find instructions on the Internet on how to do this. Even using regular craft paint will give your eggs a more unique look than what is commercially available, and using paintbrushes to decorate eggs allows for more creativity than just setting an egg in a cup to soak some color into its shell.

Some Neopagan traditions focus more on the equinox aspect. The old-fashioned balance scale can be used as a symbol as it is a time when night and day are in balance with one another. It is also a time to work on evaluating your own life and putting it into balance. In the magickal aspect of the equinox, all things come into balance at this time, not just the night and day or light and dark. Everything and its counterpart come together in balance and harmony; yin and yang. We make the switch from the passive half of the year to the active half of the year. The dark half of the year deals often with death and decay, but the light half brings life and growth. Workings move from being inner workings to outward workings. During the dark half of the year, our lives contract and shrink, and we tend to live in what seems to be a smaller world as we stay inside more often, don't travel as much, and generally spend less time with people outside of those who live in our homes. Now with the equinox and the new light and soon-to-be longer days, our lives expand and grow, the world becomes larger again as we travel farther away from home, and we make more plans to be outdoors and to do new things and visit new places.

Still others see the equinox as the true beginning of the sun's power over the night. After today there will be more sun than darkness until the Autumnal Equinox. Therefore it is a celebration of the light's victory over the dark. Sun symbols are often a part of this celebration that remind of us of the sun's growing strength and that we too can grow in strength each day if we just decide to work on doing that ourselves. Sometimes when we try to make positive changes in our lives and work on ourselves, it helps to know there are others in the same boat as us doing the same thing. At the equinox, not only are other people working to become stronger, the sun itself is as well. We aren't alone in our quest to become stronger, we have one of the greatest allies working right alongside of us.

Honey and maple syrup are two other symbols used at Ostara. Both can be used as offerings to whatever deities you are working with. In the spring, the bees wake from their hibernation and honey production begins again. Also in the spring, as the days warm the sap begins running in the trees again. The trees can be tapped and the sap collected can be boiled down into syrup. Sugar maples are the best trees to make syrup from, though it is possible to make it from other maples as well.

While you may not want to raise your own bees or tap your own trees, or even have trees to tap, honey and syrup can easily be picked up at just about any store. Health food stores will also offer organic versions of each. Pouring honey or syrup into the ground around gardening areas makes an excellent offering to the deities to ensure a fertile plot and a bountiful harvest later on. If you are someone who likes to work with the fey, bowls of honey and syrup can also be left out as gifts to them.

The butterfly is another symbol of Ostara. Butterflies go through a great transformation in order to exist. As a furry little caterpillar, it cocoons itself until spring, when it is able to fight its way out of the cocoon and spread its wings to enjoy its new life. The butterfly works as a symbol in a couple different regards. First of all, the butterfly can be compared to the god who is preparing to be reborn. The cocoon is the womb of the goddess where the god waits until it is time for him to come forth. The butterfly also works as a symbol for any of those of us who have projects that are related to starting anew. The butterfly gets to start a completely different life when it emerges from its cocoon, (and in this one it even gets the chance to have a life with wings!). When we burst out of the cocoon of winter, we can choose to start our lives over in any way we want as well. (We might not be able to get wings, but you get the idea.) We are coming out of our own cocoon and are ready to spread our own figurative wings and soar.

The lamb is another baby animal that holds a strong significance for Ostara. We are entering the first zodiac sign, Aries, which is of course represented by the ram. The lamb can be seen as the young god who will someday become a strong, powerful ram. Male sheep will butt their heads and horns together, just like their goat relatives, to show who is the strongest. In both recent and ancient history, the lamb was often a sacrifice to the gods. In Jewish lore, it was the blood of the lamb that had to be placed on the doorway during Passover to keep their sons safe from being killed. In Christian lore, the sacrificed lamb is connected to Jesus Christ who is often called "the lamb of God," meaning the sacrifice of God. The lamb has been associated with this time of year for thousands of years.

While Christians and followers of some gods saw this as a time of sacrifice, that generally is not the mood in most Pagan celebrations. We deal with sacrifice on the opposite side of the wheel. Our focus now is on the returning light and the renewed life that came because of the previous sacrifice, but the sacrifice itself is not the main point. Instead, we focus heavily on those aspects of renewal, resurrection, rejuvenation, and rebirth. We are looking forward into the future. The past is done and behind us and nothing can change it anymore, we can only move forward and decide what our actions will be from here on out. We can't go back and change the way things were done in the past, we must simply learn to accept them, live with them, whether good or bad, right or wrong, and use our past experiences to help shape our future choices and decisions.

SPELLS
AND
DIVINATION

e beginnings, birth, renewal, rejuvenation, balance, fertility, chang

strength, vernal equinox, sun enters Aries, Libra in the Fa

Green Man, Amalthea, Aphrodite, Blodeuwedd, Eostre, E

a, Flora, Freya, Gaia, Guinevere, Persephone, Libera, A

npet, Umaj, Vila, Aengus MacOg, Cernunnos, Herma, Tha

Kama, Mabon Osiris, Pan, Thor, abundance, growth, health, e

al healing, patience understanding virtue, spring, honor, contentn

hic abilities, spiritual truth, intuition, receptivity, love, inner s

provement, spiritual awareness, purification, childhood, innocenc

bly, creativity, communication, concentration, divination, harm

abilities, prosperity, attraction, blessings, happiness, luck, mone

ty, guidance, visions, insight, family, wishes, celebrating life cy

iendship, courage, attracts love, honesty, good health, emotions

improvement, influence, motivation, peace, rebirth, self preserv

nine power, freedom, optimism, new beginnings, vernal equino

creation, sun, apple blossom, columbine, crocus, daffodil, dais

sy, honeysuckle, jasmine, jonquil, lilac, narcissus, orange blosso

nrose, rose, the fool, the magician, the priestess, justice, the sta

s, gathering, growth, abundance, eggs, seeds, honey, dill, winter

$\mathcal{L}$IKE ALL SABBATS, each one lends itself as the ideal time to work with different energies to bring about change. When it comes right down to it, a spell is simply a way of making change occur, so the spells in this section are going to deal with helping make certain changes manifest in your life that work with the energies of Ostara and the equinox. We will also look at what types of questions it is a good time to be asking in your divination work.

While Ostara is about new beginnings, sometimes starting over is one of the hardest things we can ever imagine doing. Whether it's starting a new job, starting a life without a spouse or a significant other, or maybe even starting a life with a new spouse or significant other, change is hard—even when the change is for the better. Sometimes even though we know something may be for the best, that doesn't make it any easier to deal with it. Most of us fight against change, it's a natural instinct, which often doesn't get us anywhere but frustrated. Even when the change is something we want, it can be difficult to adjust to it, but when the change is something we don't want, it can feel downright suffocating to have to do something we have to do but don't want to do.

This candle spell is going to help relax the mind enough to open it to the new possibilities this new change may present, and therefore it will also make you more accepting of the change that is taking place.

Spell to Assist in Difficult Changes

You will need two candles for this spell, one black and one blue, and something to light them with. You will also need a place where you can be alone, cast a circle, and be at about eye level with the flame of your candles. This should be a safe location to burn candles, where you won't be in danger of falling asleep. If at all possible, you should perform this spell outside.

Set the two candles next to each other, black on the left and blue on the right. Cast your circle as you normally would and then either sit or stand in front of the two candles.

Take a moment to take several deep breaths and to empty your mind of all other thoughts, particularly if you are already stressed about the change you are here to work on. Relax as much as you can while still focusing on what the problem is, but feel yourself getting distance from it.

Light the black candle. As you do so, say either aloud or to yourself the following:

The confusion, hurt, and stress I feel
burn away inside this flame.
The change I face is made for me;
no other can take my pain.

Spend some time staring into the flame of the candle. Project your hurt, sadness, confusion, stress, anger, and any negative emotions you have regarding this change into the flame of that candle. Imagine those feelings burning up in the flame and turning into nothing but smoke that disappears into the air. Spend as much time as you need doing this. When you think you are done, take a few moments to just relax. See if any more of those feelings come to the surface, and if they do, go back to projecting them back into the candle. Give yourself a couple of breaks and do a "stress check" each time you do. Once you can tell you really do feel a bit better, go ahead and move on to the next part of the spell.

Light the blue candle and say:

Moving forward, moving on,
changes must be made.
The past is gone, it slips away
from my mind to fade.
The future is what matters now.
I need my strength so bold,

to make the changes I must make
and let them take ahold.

Now stare into the flame of the blue candle. Imagine positive reactions and results from whatever these changes are. Keep anything negative out. If a negative thought creeps in, turn back to the black candle and send it into that flame instead. Keep all of your positive thoughts going into the flame of the blue candle, where they are absorbed by the flame and then dispersed into the universe. Keep the negative thoughts going into the black candle, where they are burned up and destroyed. Go back and forth between both candles as much as you feel necessary. When all the negative emotions are gone and you feel ready to take on this new challenge, move back to the black candle and say:

Negative feelings, I don't need you.
I cleanse you and release you into the air.

Blow the black candle out, allowing the feelings to just float off and away. Next move back to the blue candle and say:

These changes I make are for the best.
I accept you and release you into my surroundings.

Blow the blue candle out gently, allowing the positive energy to stay in the room with you and permeate the air.

You may need to perform this spell several times over to fully rid yourself of the negative feelings associated with the change you have to make. Small changes won't take as long, but harder, more difficult changes may need you to perform this spell nightly for a couple of weeks until you feel you have things more under control. Then you can cut down to once a week, once every other week, finally to once a month, and then only if you feel those feeling trying to creep back in again. If you have more than one change going on at a time, you can work on those at the same time, just be careful not to overwhelm yourself, particularly in the beginning. If it starts to feel like it's too much to deal with at once, then break those changes down into separate sessions until you are strong enough to tackle them all at once, and work your way back up to combining them as you work at chipping them away. For example, by the time you get down to once a month, you should be able to combine several together if need be and work on them all at the same time. If you can't do that many at once though, don't worry about it. Everyone handles stress differently, so make sure you do what works best for you.

Spell to Restore Balance to Your Life

Often our lives get completely hectic and out of control. For many people this happens during the winter holidays and getting life back in balance again may seem impossible. We don't eat right. We don't sleep right. We might not be getting enough exercise. We may have let our spirituality slip to the back burner. We may have let many things slip to the back burner. While this spell can be done at any time, it's very well suited for the spring for its renewal connections. It's also extremely well suited for the equinox for its restoring balance aspect. What better day to restore balance to your own life than on the day that is naturally all about balance to begin with.

For this spell, you will need to gather a few things ahead of time. You will need to create a powdered incense mixture out of a few different herbs and resins, so you will also need a mortar and pestle, a fireproof container (your cauldron perhaps), two charcoal tablets, and a lighter. The herbs and resins you need are angelica, basil, sage, sweet woodruff, vervain, yarrow, comfrey, chamomile, frankincense, and myrrh. You won't need a lot, just a teaspoon of each is fine for now, or you could do a tablespoon of each to save some for future recharging.

You will also need two pieces of amber. They may be stones of amber or amber set into a piece of jewelry—earrings would be ideal since there would be two and they go on each side of the body, creating balance. You could also use two rings (one for each hand) or two bracelets (one for each wrist), but try to avoid using a necklace if you can. If you are using jewelry, gold is preferred to silver in this case. You will be able to perform this spell again anytime you need to recharge, using the same amber pieces or jewelry. You will also need two green candles.

Begin by collecting all of your ingredients. You may also want to create a circle in which you do your prep work, but that is entirely up to you. Some people are able to do their prep work and their actual workings all in one location, others not, so just do whatever works best for you. Using the mortar and pestle, crush all of the herbs and resins together. It's not very easy to crush resins, so some people use electric chopper/grinders just for this purpose. (If you go this route, be sure you have a separate one for your magickal workings. Don't use the same one you use for food to prevent cross-contamination in either direction, both physically and magickally.)

When your incense is complete, set up your altar area with your fireproof container in the center with a dish containing the incense next to it and the amber stone on the opposite side. Place a green candle on each side of the fireproof container, creating balance. Cast your circle if you didn't prior to preparing the incense, and call in any deities you prefer to work with. Light the charcoal tablets in your fireproof container (you are using two since this spell is about balance and also because it really helps in the burning of incense. If you only use one charcoal tablet, you have a much smaller burning area and often a lot of the incense will just sit in the cauldron and not be burned). Allow the charcoal time to fully turn red and become coated in ash.

Light the green candle on the left side of the altar and say:

Sometimes life slips out of control.
It is for me to set it right—
to strike a balance on this day
of equal day and night.

Light the green candle on the right side of the altar and repeat:

Sometimes life slips out of control.
It is for me to set it right—
to strike a balance on this day
of equal day and night.

Then add:

As I light these candles,
one on each side,
I begin my journey back.
Restoring balance

step by step,
putting my life back on track.

Take a small pinch of the incense and sprinkle it on top of the lit charcoal tablets. As you do so say:

Return balance to my life,
and create a harmony
that all parts of my life
live together in symmetry.
With these intentions
charge this stone,
so that my life
takes a balanced tone.

As the smoke rises into the air, take a piece of your amber and pass it through the smoke slowly in a clockwise circular motion. Sprinkle the incense with your nondominant hand and hold the amber with your dominant hand.

We often work in threes when doing magick, but because this particular spell is about balance, we want to keep everything about the spell nice and balanced as well. So, instead of using three pinches of incense and saying the above a total of three times, we are going to do everything six times. This way we are still using a multiple of three, and yet we are keeping it balanced with an even number and not off balance with an odd number.

After you say the above once and have made your circle through the smoke, use another pinch of incense and make another pass with the amber. Continue doing this until you have done it a total of six times. After finishing with the first piece of amber, replace it on your altar and repeat the entire process with the second piece.

When you finish six rounds with the second piece, place it back on your altar as well.

Pick up the candle on the right-hand side and hold it close enough to your mouth to blow out. Say:

> *The magick done here today*
> *sets in motion*
> *a brand new way.*
> *I pull together from all of my sides,*
> *to balance out*
> *as the chaos dies.*
> *I release this magick into the air*
> *so mote it be*
> *into the Goddess's care.*

Slowly blow out the flame of the candle and envision the magick being released and swirling in the air on its journey out into the universe. Pick up the candle on the left side of the altar and repeat exactly as with the first candle, reciting the above, blowing out the flame, and envisioning the magick being released into the universe. Close your circle.

Dispose of the ashes from your fireproof container. If you have a stream nearby this would be the most ideal place to dump them, but you can also bury them. If there are still pieces of herbs or resins that did not burn, bury it in a location where you won't be planting anything. Some people keep a small section of yard (a couple square feet) or a special planter with just dirt in it for burying their magickal workings. Wear the jewelry to help bring your life into balance. If you used amber gems, keep one in your pockets on each side of your body to keep them balanced against one another. If you feel it is needed, you can repeat this spell at the Autumnal Equinox as well.

Spring Is in the Air Love Attraction Spell

With spring and love buzzing all around the air, this spell is literally like sticking a butterfly net right into the middle of the swirl to see what you can catch. It isn't about seeing one particular butterfly and chasing it down, it's about putting the net out there and seeing which one is curious enough to come check it out. This spell is best done outside, as it will make a little bit of a mess and because you want to send your intent out as far and wide as you can.

For this spell you will need both red and pink glitter—at least half a cup of each, but more if you can do more. (Red for love, lust, passion, and courage; pink for compassion, tenderness, harmony, affection, and love, too.) You will also need a couple of fresh red and pink roses.

To prepare for the ritual, carefully peel each petal off of the roses and put them into a large bowl. Next add the glitter and gently mix the two up a bit with your hands. You don't want to damage or bruise the rose petals and the glitter will stay pretty much separated, but if you can get at least a few of the rose petals to have some glitter stick to them that is good. If you want, before adding the glitter, spritz a little water on the rose petals to help the glitter stick.

Once you are prepared, cast a circle calling in either the Greek gods Aphrodite and Eros or their Roman equivalents Venus and Cupid.

Hold the bowl out in front of you and say:

(Name your chosen deities),
bless these petals and infuse them with your power.
Help them to help me in my search for love this hour.
Find the one that's meant for me and send them on their way,
to come into my life and to become what may.

You will notice that in this spell we are not asking for a specific person nor a specific trait. We are asking the god and goddess we are entrusting to find who they deem appropriate to fit the bill and to give that person a shove in the right direction. Love spells should never be done asking for a specific person to fall in love with you. This goes against the person's free will and is simply unethical. Cupid and Eros know what they are doing, and they will direct their arrows to where they need to go.

This is the part of the spell that gets fun even if you feel a little silly doing it. It is spring, love is in the air and that means being a little silly is perfectly fine! You will continue to repeat the last two lines of this spell:

Find the one that's meant for me and send them on their way,
to come into my life and to become what may.

As you recite these two lines, dance around, scoop up handfuls of petals and glitter, and throw them as high as you can into the air. You will most likely get covered with glitter, but hey, it is glitter, so it's all good. Throw the petals and glitter in all directions: up, north, south, east, west. Spin and throw it, just toss it really good all over the place. When you are finished say:

(Name your chosen deities),
in your names, I ask for this love to be brought to me.
If it pleases you as well, so mote it be.

Close your circle. You will probably also want to wash your clothes and take a shower!

Blessing Eggs

Like the cascarones, blessing eggs are blown out eggs refilled with herbs, oils, and whatever you want to symbolize a blessing you either want to receive or give to someone else. To begin, make two holes in the egg, one at each end. One can be small but the other will need to be large enough to fill the egg back up (but still try to keep it small). Blow into the small hole, pushing the yoke and white out the larger hole into a bowl. Once empty, carefully rinse the egg out. Using the Ostara correspondences at the back of this book, choose herbs, flowers, oils, and even colored glittered that represent what it is you are looking for. For example, if you need to make more money at your career, you may want to include green glitter and oak moss. If you are making an egg for a loved one who has difficulty sleeping, try blue glitter and lavender.

Fill the egg up as much as you can and use a small piece of masking tape to cover the larger hole on the end. Next, you should paint and decorate the egg to also correspond with the blessing you want to receive or give. You can use regular craft paints to paint the eggs and add words, symbols, or runes to the egg to boost its power. For example, an egg for money can be painted green and you can add the words *money* and *abundance* as well as a $.

Once the eggs are finished, place them on your altar during your Ostara ritual. Take a moment during your ritual to ask your deities to bless the eggs and yourself (or loved one) with what it is you are asking for. If you have made the egg for someone else, give it to them after you have completed your ritual. Both you and your loved one may then decide if you want to display your eggs in a location where you will often see it, or "plant" it so the blessings may grow by burying it somewhere—this can be in a vegetable or flower garden or even just in a planter if you don't have room for a garden. If you want, you can even make two identical eggs—one to be displayed so you are reminded of what it is you asked for, and one to be planted so that it can grow.

Egg Cleansing and Divination

This cleansing is easier to do if you have the help of someone else, however, you can still do it on your own. Begin by filling a clear glass with blessed water or moon water. Place it on your altar and add a few drops of your favorite protection oil. Place a fresh, unbroken egg on your altar as well. You may want to place it on a piece of material, such as a scarf, to keep it from rolling.

Cast your circle and invite your deities in. Hold the glass of water in your hands and ask your deities for protection, for cleansing, and to assist you in seeing clearly. Place the glass back on your altar and then do the same with the egg. Also while holding the egg, ask your deities to allow it to absorb any and all negativity.

Once you are done, take the egg and roll it around the crown of your head. Next roll it down your face, neck, each arm, your chest, torso, back, and the front and back of each leg. Finally, roll the egg over each palm and the soles of each foot. Always make sure you are rolling the egg downward toward the ground. This is where it comes in handy to have help! If working with a partner, lie down while he or she rolls the egg all over your body, turn over and have them repeat the process. When it's their turn, do the same for them (with a fresh egg, of course!)

After rolling the egg all over your body, immediately crack the egg and pour the contents into the water. Take a moment to observe the egg. Pay attention to the smell, color, any shape it takes, and whether or not there is blood present. A bad odor, blood, or cloudy water is a sign of a problem and more cleansing and protection work should be done.

Look carefully into the yolk, if any of these other signs are present, a face may appear in the yolk. It is the face of the person who harbors ill will against you. You need to be careful of this person, forgive them, and work your cleansings and protections.

If an eye appears in the yolk, this is the infamous "evil eye," and again you need to work your cleansings and protections. You can perform the egg cleansing several times until the egg comes out normal looking.

If you see small bubbles in the water, this means your guardians have been at work for you and have already taken care of the problem. Be sure to send them thanks and then reset your protections.

If the water is clear, no blood is present, and there is no foul or bad smell, there haven't been any magickal workings against you. Go ahead and reset your protections and thank your deities for their assistance and protection. No matter what you find in your egg, take it outside and bury it in the ground. This should not be done in a planter unless it is an extremely large one as not only will it possibly start to smell, animals such as opossums, raccoons, or even coyotes may be drawn to the smell and dig it up.

Divination by Oomancy

This practice is the art of divining with eggs and comes from the Greek words *oon for* "egg" and *manteia* for "divination." It is also known as ooscopy, oomancia, oomantia, ooscopia, ovamancy, or ovomancy.

The most common type of egg divination begins by separating the whites from the yolk and then quickly pouring the white into very hot water and interpreting the shapes that form. The best way to do this is to bring the water to a rolling boil and then remove it from the heat, allowing the bubbling to cease before quickly adding the whites. How you interpret the shapes you see is entirely up to you, but remember to keep an open mind and don't just see what you want to see. This is also a good divination to do with a partner so you can bounce ideas and interpretations off of each other. What one may see as a dollar sign, another may see as a snake.

Another form of divination with eggs is to tell whether a mother is having a single baby or multiples. Take a fresh egg and rub it on the mother's pregnant belly for a few minutes, then crack the egg into a bowl. The number of yolks predicts how many babies the mother will have. This can be a scary divination for some people, particularly if there is blood in the egg or if the yolk is broken. These are signs of a miscarriage or some other problem with the birth.

Divination by Floromancy

Using flowers in divination is called floromancy. While there are several different types of floromancy, not all of them have specific names, such as this version below. Not everyone will be able to do this divination, it depends on where you live and what the local vegetation and flora is like. It's easy enough to do, however, and may be more likely to happen if you are a person who takes a lot of walks. All you have to do is look for the first spring flower and know the day of the week. If you see the first spring flower on a Sunday, it means you will have very good luck for the next several weeks. If you see it on a Monday, you will have good luck throughout the spring season. If on Tuesday you find your first flower of spring, whatever you attempt, you will succeed. If the first flower is found on a Wednesday, a marriage is coming. (It doesn't necessarily mean yours!) The flower on Thursday is a warning of financial troubles, while one on Friday predicts wealth. The first spring flower on a Saturday is bad luck.

In order to do this divination correctly you really must look for flowers every day. You can't just go out on Fridays looking for flowers and then say, "Oooooh, I'm going to be wealthy!" It doesn't work like that. (Though wouldn't it be great if it were only that easy?)

Divination by Daphnomancy

Daphnomancy combines pyromancy with bay laurel leaves to predict the future. You will need fresh (not dried) leaves for this type of divination and either a fireproof container or an open fire of some sort (bonfire or fireplace). If you use a fireproof container such as a cauldron, you can use a couple of charcoal tablets as your fire source. Get the tablets lit and brightly glowing before adding a few leaves, or go ahead and throw them into an open fire while thinking of your question. If the leaves catch fire and crackle as they burn, it means the timing is favorable. If the flames smolder, suffocate, and die out, or the leaves burn silently without crackling, the timing is not favorable. Flames rising together is a good sign. If there is only one flame point, it means you are being single-minded, or you may need to be single-minded. If two flame points are visible, you are going to need the help of a friend. If three flame points burn, your outcome will have an amicable conclusion.

Sitting around a bonfire taking turns reading the burning leaves for yourself, family, and/or friends can be a fun way to spend your equinox evening. Not to mention, the burning of the leaves smells pretty good.

A Spring Tarot Spread for Coming Changes

This tarot spread is a quick and easy way to get some input on what kind of changes are in store for you this spring. It doesn't matter what type of tarot deck you use, just make sure you start off by making sure it is shuffled extremely well, particularly if it is a new deck. Cut the deck into three piles and then choose which pile you want on top, in the middle, and then on the bottom. Choose a total of eight cards, two columns with four cards in each column. Work left to right when placing the cards down (not top to bottom). The four cards on the left will be major changes or challenges. The cards on the right will give you information about the outcome for each of the changes. If you have questions regarding the changes or the outcomes, you can use additional cards as clarifiers until you feel you have enough information.

When doing card readings or other types of divination at this time of year, you want to focus on certain questions that tie in with the energies of the season. Asking about changes and new beginnings are a good idea. Are you looking to start a new project or job but you're not sure if it's the right time? Consult the cards or another divination source with these types of questions. Other topics to ask about right now would be anything related to gardening, fertility, growth, life, light, love, or any other type of rebirth or renewal. There are a ton of different types of oracle cards on the market these days—animal guides, angel message cards, fairy message cards—everyone has some type of message for you. Use some of these decks to find out more about bringing balance into your life and the changes you should be making. Message cards are ideal for these purposes, often more so than tarot cards, as you tend to get an even more direct answer.

Use this time of renewal and rebirth to get yourself straightened out, in balance, and on the right path to a happy, healthy life.

RECIPES
AND
CRAFTS

beginnings, birth, renewal, rejuvenation, balance, fertility, chang
strength, vernal equinox, sun enters Aries, Libra in the Sou
Green Man, Amalthea, Aphrodite, Blodeuwedd, Eostre, E
, Flora, Freya, Gaia, Guinevere, Persephone, Libera, A
npet, Umaj, Vila, Aengus MacOg, Cernunnos, Herma, The
ama, Mabon Osiris, Pan, Thor, abundance, growth, health, ea
l healing, patience understanding virtue, spring, honor, contentn
hic abilities, spiritual truth, intuition, receptivity, love, inner se
provement, spiritual awareness, purification, childhood, innocence
ty, creativity, communication, concentration, divination, harmo
bilities, prosperity, attraction, blessings, happiness, luck, money
, guidance, visions, insight, family, wishes, celebrating life cyc
endship, courage, attracts love, honesty, good health, emotions,
improvement, influence, motivation, peace, rebirth, self preserva
mine power, freedom, optimism, new beginnings, vernal equino
creation, sun, apple blossom, columbine, crocus, daffodil, daisy
ry, honeysuckle, jasmine, jonquil, lilac, narcissus, orange blossom,
rose, rose, the fool, the magician, the priestess, justice, the sta
, gathering, growth, abundance, eggs, seeds, honey, dill, aspara

*W*HILE PREPARING FOR the sabbats may be a lot of work, it is a lot of fun as well. Pulling ingredients and supplies together to transform them from ordinary items into tasty food and pretty decorations is its very own kind of magick.

Ostara Recipes

Food is often at the center of a get together. Feasting after a ritual helps to ground the participants, and it also offers a time to commune in fellowship with others. Laughing, joking, talking, and eating all go hand in hand as people enjoy themselves over a fine meal.

These recipes are sure to bring your group or family together to savor their wonderful flavors. If possible, get your entire group to cook together as well. When people prepare food together, it simply adds to the magick.

Steamed Asparagus with Lemon

Asparagus is pretty much the first plant ready to be harvested, and it's ready early in the year, so it is perfect to eat while celebrating the first day of spring,

Ingredients:
1 pound asparagus
1 lemon
Salt and pepper (optional)

Make sure to cut the hard ends off of the asparagus and place the rest in a steamer. It does not take very long to steam vegetables, so keep an eye on them. When ready, they will turn a darker green color. It will probably only take five minutes or so once the water for the steam starts boiling. If you would like the asparagus a little softer, cook it longer. While the asparagus is steaming, zest one tablespoon of lemon peel and then juice the lemon and mix the juice and zest together. Drain the water off of the asparagus and pour the lemon mixture over the asparagus. Lightly salt and pepper if you wish.

Stuffed Eggs with Stone Ground Mustard

Hard-boiled eggs are a must for an Ostara celebration. Try this twist on traditional deviled eggs.

Ingredients:
1 dozen hard-boiled eggs, cooled and peeled
4 teaspoons finely chopped scallions
4 teaspoons finely chopped celery
4 teaspoons stone ground mustard
½ cup mayonnaise
Curry powder to taste

Slice cooled and peeled hard-boiled eggs in half lengthwise. Scoop yolk out into a bowl and mash. Add scallions, celery, mustard, and mayonnaise to the yolks and mix well. Spoon filling back into each egg half. Top with a sprinkle of curry powder.

Grecian Goddess Quiche

Ingredients:

6 eggs

½ cup milk

2 tablespoons chopped red onion

¼ cup chopped black olives

½ cup chopped Roma tomatoes

¾ cup precooked spinach

½ cup chopped red peppers

¾ cup crumbled feta cheese

1 teaspoon chopped fresh oregano

1 teaspoon chopped fresh basil

Salt and pepper to taste

1 frozen (ready-to-bake) piecrust

Preheat oven to 400°F. In a bowl, lightly beat the eggs. Add in milk and beat for another minute. Add in all other ingredients and mix well. Pour the egg mixture into the crust and ensure that the pieces of vegetables and cheese are equally spread out throughout the crust. Bake for 35 minutes. Check to make sure quiche is firm in the center before removing from oven.

Mint Lamb Chops

Ingredients:
½ cup olive oil
½ cup chopped fresh mint
1 tablespoons minced garlic
Salt and pepper to taste
4 lamb chops

Combine olive oil, mint, garlic, salt, and pepper in a casserole dish. Add lamb chops and marinate for 20 minutes. Flip chops over and marinate for another 20 minutes. Place chops on a broiler pan, coating well with the mint mixture. Broil chops on each side for about 6 minutes.

Hot Cross Buns

Ingredients:

4 cups flour

1 package active dry yeast

1½ teaspoons ground cinnamon

¾ cup milk

½ cup vegetable oil

⅓ cup sugar

½ teaspoon salt

3 eggs

1 cup raisins

Icing:

1 egg white, beaten

1 cup powdered sugar

1 tablespoon milk

1 teaspoon vanilla

Combine 1½ cups flour, yeast, and cinnamon in a large bowl. In a saucepan with a candy thermometer, combine milk, oil, sugar, and salt and heat it to 120°F. Once heated, pour mixture into flour mixture and then add the eggs. Beat on low to blend, scraping sides of bowl, then beat on high for 3 more minutes.

Using a spatula, fold in raisins. Add in the rest of the flour. When it gets too thick to work with a spoon, pour out onto a lightly floured surface and knead with your hands. Shape into a ball and place in a lightly greased bowl. Cover with a dishtowel and let rise for 90 minutes. Dough should about double in size.

Punch the dough down and place back onto a floured surface, cover, and let sit for another 10 minutes. Divide the dough into 12 to 15 portions, and roll each portion into a ball. Place the dough balls two inches apart on a greased cookie sheet. Cover with a towel and let rise again for 45 minutes. Using a sharp knife, make a crisscross cut into the top of each bun. Brush each bun with egg white. Bake at 375°F for 12 to 14 minutes.

While the buns are baking, mix up the icing by adding all ingredients in a bowl and beating with a mixer. Add more milk if you need to thin it to drizzling consistency.

Allow buns to cool for about 10 minutes before drizzling the icing on top of them.

Honey Cake

Anything made with honey is great to have at Ostara as the bees have woken up from their hibernation and are busy buzzing around and getting the honey made. Dishes with honey celebrate the awakening of the bees and the awakening of the plant life the bees depend on in order to make their honey.

Ingredients:
2½ cups flour
3 teaspoons baking powder
½ teaspoon baking soda
½ teaspoon salt
1 cup sugar
2 teaspoons cinnamon
1 cup honey
⅓ cup vegetable oil
4 eggs
1 teaspoon orange zest
1 cup orange juice

Preheat oven to 350°F and grease and flour two round eight- or nine-inch cake pans. Blend all dry ingredients together and then add all wet ingredients, mixing well. Pour into pans and bake for approximately 28 minutes. Check centers of cakes with a toothpick and remove from oven when the toothpick comes out clean. Allow cakes to cool in pans for 5 minutes and then turn out onto wire racks.

Ham and Parsley Sauce

Parsley is another early herb that has many uses. From cleansing the palate, to decorations, to a staple herb, parsley does it all. This Irish parsley sauce drizzled over a cooked ham is just the thing for a beautiful spring day.

Ingredients:
A ham

For the sauce:
¼ cup butter
¼ cup flour
1¼ cup light cream
1 bunch of fresh parsley finely chopped
Salt and pepper to taste

Bake your ham in the oven, following the recommended time and temperature. A few minutes before it is done, start the parsley sauce. Melt the butter in a pan and add the flour to make a roux. Stir constantly so it doesn't burn, and cook for several minutes. With the heat on low, slowly add the cream and continue stirring constantly until the roux is completely blended in. Stir in the parsley, salt, and pepper, and allow to simmer for 4 to 5 minutes while continually stirring. Remove from heat and serve heavily drizzled over sliced ham.

Cheesy Dill Mashed Potatoes

Dill is a great herb to associate with spring. It is a quick-growing herb that slightly resembles the asparagus plant. It has a fresh green taste to it as well.

Ingredients:
4 cups mashed potatoes (you can cheat and use instant)
8 ounces softened cream cheese
1 egg, beaten
2 tablespoons dried dill

Grease a two-quart casserole dish and preheat the oven to 350°F. Using a hand mixer, combine the mashed potatoes, cream cheese, egg, and dill. Whip it until the cream cheese is fully incorporated and smooth. Use a spatula to transfer the mixture into the greased pan, smoothing the top out. Bake for 45 minutes.

Grasshopper

For the adults, this rich and minty alcoholic beverage is a perfect accompaniment to Ostara. Its light green color blends in well with the colors of the season, and its minty taste is cool and refreshing. Even the name evokes feelings of spring and the outdoors. The grasshopper can be made in a blender with ice cubes to make it a frozen drink or in a shaker on the rocks.

Ingredients:

1 part cream

1 part white crème de cacao

1 part crème de menthe

Mix all three parts together in a shaker and pour over ice in a martini glass. Or add mixture to a blender with ice cubes and blend until smooth for a frozen drink.

Kids' Spring Green Punch

This punch can be made up for kids to have their own cool green drink.

Ingredients:

8 cans guanabana nectar (or guava and banana
    nectars separately)

4 cans 7UP soda

1 quart green sherbet

Mix all ingredients together into a punch bowl and serve.

While many of the previous recipes are considered traditional foods for this time of year, several of them do not go very well with the more contemporary diets often enjoyed by Pagans, such as vegan, vegetarian, or pescatarian. They may not be options for those who simply like to eat a more sustainable localized diet.

Asparagus is a spring vegetable, as well as lettuce, mushrooms, and radishes. These vegetables grow quickly, and they grow better in cooler temperatures than hotter ones. These few vegetables can be combined into soups, salads, and many other dishes. Another spring, and often local, food item is fish. With the warming of lakes and rivers, fish become more active and hungry, and therefore more easily caught. If you are an angler yourself, you know just how true this is. If you visit farmers' markets or food co-ops, fresh fish are highly in season, and often at a good price.

The following recipes are for those looking for menu suggestions that fit in vegan, vegetarian, or pescatarian diets.

Raw Asparagus and Avocado Soup

If you aren't used to eating raw foods, this will be a bit different for you, but this thick soup is filled with flavor and is healthy and rather inexpensive to make as well.

Ingredients:
1 pound asparagus
2 avocados
½ teaspoon salt
¼ teaspoon pepper
3 cups water

Cut the hard ends off of the asparagus and throw them away. Finely chop about ¼ of the asparagus tips and set aside. Chop the rest of the asparagus into pieces about half an inch long and place in a blender. Cut the avocados in half, remove the pits, and slice the flesh into small pieces. Scoop the avocado pieces out and add them to the blender. Add salt, pepper, and water to the blender and purée until smooth. Add the reserved pieces of chopped asparagus tips and chill for at least 30 minutes before serving.

Honey Ginger Carrots

Ingredients:

2 teaspoons ground ginger

3 tablespoons honey

2 tablespoons olive oil

1 orange

1 pound baby carrots

Use a slow cooker to make this delicious side dish. In a small bowl, mix together the ginger, honey, and olive oil. Zest and juice one orange and add to the mixture. Mix well and make sure the ginger doesn't make any lumps. Pour scrubbed and trimmed baby carrots into the slow cooker and pour liquid mixture all over the top, mixing well to make sure all the carrots are covered. Cook on low for several hours until the carrots are tender.

Garlic Mushrooms

With the melting of the snow and the coming of the rain, the mushrooms will soon be out in full force, so any spring meal is the perfect time to include them. This recipe will make for a large pot of mushrooms and comes out even better if you can cook it slowly all day out in a cauldron over an open fire.

Ingredients:
3 pounds mushrooms
1 large onion
1 head of garlic
1 bunch fresh parsley
4 tablespoons butter (or non-dairy substitute for vegans)
2 cups Chablis wine

Clean the mushrooms and cut off the stems. Peel and slice the onion into at least quarters if not eighths—you do want large chunks, but not too terribly large. Peel the entire head of garlic and either dice or use a garlic press to crush it. Finely chop the parsley.

Using a large pot, melt the butter over medium-low heat. Add in the onions and cook until they are translucent. Add in the wine, garlic, and parsley and mix well. Add in the mushrooms and mix everything together. Cover them and let the mushrooms cook for a couple of hours on low heat.

Honey Lime Scallops

Ingredients:

1 lime

3 tablespoons honey

1 pound of scallops

Zest and juice the lime and add both to the honey, blending very well. Stir mixture with the scallops, making sure the scallops are completely covered. Place under broiler until scallops are cooked all the way through. Broiling time will vary depending on the size of the scallops.

Thai Chili Fish and Peppers

This wonderfully tasty and slightly spicy fish dish will awaken your taste buds for spring.

Ingredients:
1 red pepper
1 orange pepper
1 yellow pepper
1 small bottle Thai chili sauce
4 fish fillets such as tilapia or whatever is local for you

Preheat oven to 350 degrees. Finely slice each of the peppers into small, thin strips. Mix them together in a bowl and add enough chili sauce to thoroughly cover the peppers. Place the fish into a pan and spoon the peppers over the top, making sure the fish is completely covered. Bake until the fish is white and flaky. Baking time will vary depending on the thickness of the fish fillets.

Egg Drop Soup

Ingredients:

¼ cup scallions finely chopped

1 tablespoon ground ginger

6 cups vegetable broth

1 dozen eggs

1 tablespoon cornstarch

¼–½ cup cold water

Add scallions, ginger, and broth to a pot and allow to boil. While waiting for the broth to heat, crack open all of the eggs into a mixing bowl. Beat with a mixer or a whisk until they are well blended. In a separate cup, mix cornstarch and cold water; stir until dissolved and well blended. Once the broth is at a rolling boil, gently and slowly pour the egg into the broth, keeping the bowl moving at all times as if drizzling the egg in. If the broth stops boiling, stop pouring and allow the water to heat back up to the rolling boil. Once all of the egg has been poured in, slowly pour the cornstarch mixture into the boiling soup and stir. Allow to boil for 3 minutes to thicken up the soup.

Crafts

Ostara crafts are a fun way to be creative with your group or family during this holiday season. Spring is a wonderful time to begin new projects as well. Have fun and let the creativity flow with these fun projects.

Cascarones

Homemade cascarones can be filled with whatever you can fit into them. Glitter or chalk powder can make them a whole lot of fun and a huge mess, which makes them great for outdoor use.

You will need:

- Hollowed out whole eggshells, either real or papier-mâché
- Filling (glitter, chalk powder, confetti, herbs, etc.)
- Decorations (paint or dye, markers, stickers, etc.)
- Small funnel made of paper to fill eggs
- Tape or glue to close after filling (optional)

When making cascarones out of real eggs, there are a few tips to keep in mind. First of all, it's a lot of work. You have to poke holes in both sides of the egg and blow out all of the white and yolk, which can actually be painful, as well as a pain. Then you need to make sure you rinse them out really well so they don't start smelling bad in a couple of days. After that, you have to give them time to dry so whatever you stuff them with doesn't just stick to the inside of the shell. Another option is to use papier-mâché eggs from a craft store.

Before you fill the eggs, whether real or papier-mâché, you will want to decorate them, either with dyes, paints, stickers, or even crayons. Now would be a fun time to experiment with making natural dyes and see how that turns out. If it doesn't turn out too great, it doesn't matter too much as you are just going to smash it anyway!

Once the eggshells are decorated, you have to actually fill them with something, which means one of your holes should be large enough to get things in, while the other is still small enough to not let things out. This is why glitter and chalk dust are great materials to use. A small paper funnel rolled just right will quickly fill eggs one right after another. Fill them as full as you want. The more you fill them, the more mess you can make, which can be kind of fun!

To actually use the cascarones, you simply throw them at people. When they make contact, they will explode, covering the intended with whatever is inside (particularly glitter and chalk dust!) Be careful using real eggs, as there is a possibility of actually hurting someone this way. Broken eggshells can be very sharp and cut people, so the papier-mâché versions do offer a safety benefit. Also with the paper papier-mâché eggs,

110
......
RECIPES AND CRAFTS

you will find they have a good size hole to fill them that is often covered with a piece of thin paper. You can carefully remove this paper and add more ingredients to go along with the confetti, or remove the confetti altogether to fill completely with your own ingredients. All you have to do then is simply tape or glue the covering piece of paper back into place.

If you are making the eggs just for fun, you don't have to worry too much about things like colors or what they are filled with, but you can also use cascarones in a spiritual manner. To use them spiritually, you will need a good list of correspondences including colors, herbs, and oils. When you are preparing each cascarone with a specific person in mind, you will want to paint or dye it in colors that will have some significance for the intended. Are they in desperate need of money? Paint the shell green with dollar signs on it. Do they have trouble sleeping? Perhaps a gentle blue or a peaceful lavender with some *Zzzzzzzzs* will help do the trick. If you are making them for a lot of people, mark them with the person's name or initials, or keep a list with the person's name and a description of what their cascarone looks like. Just make sure you have some way to ensure the right cascarone ends up with the correct person.

After the cascarones are decorated with the spiritual symbols, you will need to fill them with items that correspond with the need of the person or the blessing you would like to bestow upon them. For the person in need of money, some green glitter along with some green chalk dust and a bit of oak moss would make a nice combination. For the person who can't sleep, you can mix light blue and lavender glitters and chalk dust along with some lavender buds and perhaps a little valerian.

When "bestowing" these blessings on someone, it is best to give the egg a little crack on the edge of something first and then pull it apart slowly over their head. Move it around while pouring it over them so everything doesn't dump out in one big pile. If you smash the egg directly on top of someone's head, it will hurt and you run the risk of cutting them with sharp eggshells. These will make plenty of mess, so be prepared to do it outside. You may want to provide a towel to cover people's clothes. Be prepared to do plenty of vacuuming later on because, even when done outside, a lot of ingredients will get tracked and carried back inside.

Eggshell Plant Pots

These are fun little crafts to make for people of all ages. They can also be used to decorate your altar if you like.

What you'll need:

- Eggshells—Keep as much of the egg whole as you can, breaking out just the top of the small end
- Potting soil
- Grass seed (cat grass is a good one to use)
- Paint
- Glue
- Any color pipe cleaner

Begin by making the stand for the egg out of the pipe cleaner. Wrap it in a circle several times at the bottom of the egg, giving it a little stand to set in. Glue the egg to the stand and let the glue dry. You can make all of the stands ahead of time so that when the kids or guests are ready they can just spend time decorating them and then planting the seeds.

Paint the eggshells any way you like. You can make them look like people (perhaps have a contest to see who can make their egg look the most like themselves or maybe a famous person). You can decorate them with symbols such as runes, zodiac signs, pentagrams, or any other symbols you find appropriate.

These could be used as altar decorations. They can also just be painted in solid colors. Whatever you want to do with them is up to you.

Once they are painted, they will need to dry. You may use markers to color them instead of paint to decrease the drying time, but you can get a better color choice by going with paints.

When they are all dry, use a spoon to add some potting soil to your egg planter and then add lots of the grass seed and water. Cat grass grows relatively quickly, so it shouldn't take long before you start seeing sprouts come up. Make sure to check the dampness of the soil every day to make sure they are getting enough water. With the small amount of soil in the eggs, they will dry up rather quickly.

Painted Garden Stones

Garden stones can be painted to be used as markers for what is planted in the garden or they can be used as decoration in flower gardens, fairy gardens, and smaller planters. They can line sidewalks, ponds, or birdbaths. They can also be placed just about anywhere you can think of to liven up a dull area or to make a serene location even more special and personalized.

Believe it or not, they now have premade craft kits you can buy to make these, though that seems to take away most of the fun. A premade kit really limits your creativity to what is in the kit, from the type and size of the stones to the color paint. You also won't find any other kind of embellishments that you could add if you come up with your own ideas.

If not using a kit, you'll need:

- Stones

- Outdoor paint

- Glitter and spray adhesive (optional)

- Outdoor paint sealer

You can buy small bags of tumbled stones at craft stores (usually in the floral department as they are used for weighing down vases) and at dollar stores. Those stones will be rather small in size, a couple of inches at most, but that size is good for planters or terrariums or even for altar decorations.

It may take a little more imagination to find larger stones. If you are tilling the ground to plant a garden, chances are you will find at least a few. These stones are usually rougher as they have been sitting in the ground and not exposed to the elements. Smoother stones can be found on beaches, especially if you wade out into the water a little bit. You may also find stones at riverbanks, though generally a lake will have far more. If you don't have access to any of the above, you can check with a local landscaper. You will have to pay for them of course, but it is another option. Garden markers don't need to be terribly big—fist-size usually works well. If you can get free rocks, then larger is always okay, too.

Make sure any paint you buy is marked "outdoor" paint, so you don't waste time painting only to have a rain come along and erase everything you did. You can also invest in a paint sealer (also marked "outdoor") to help the paint last even longer. If you want to add glitter, you will want an assortment of colors and a spray adhesive. Paint the rock first, then use the spray adhesive, followed by the glitter. When everything has completely dried, you will spray the sealer over everything to protect it all. You can also use rhinestones or other embellishments, but these are a lot more difficult to attach. Look for glue that is outdoor safe and does not have to be used with a porous material. Rocks just aren't very good for soaking things in!

Once you have gathered your stones and your supplies, it's time to get creative! While in the vegetable garden you may just want to mark the rows with what is in each one; you can use more than just words. If you are artistic at all, you can paint a picture of the item. Just about anyone can paint a tomato or a carrot. Most vegetables are pretty simple to paint, actually, so you can either put just the word, just the picture, or both. You can also decorate them with painted leaves or flowers as well.

Rocks in flower gardens, fairy gardens, or wherever you want can be done a bit more creatively. Maybe you want to create a peaceful feeling. A great way to do that is to paint words that help create that feeling and then decorate around them with painted flowers, glitter, or other types of embellishments.

Here are some words that can be used to help create that perfect location: serene, serenity; tranquil, tranquility; peace, peaceful, peace of mind; relax, relaxed, relaxation; Zen; Om; calm, calmness; quietude; harmony, harmonious; soothing. Or you may try: cheer; merriment; enjoy; happy, happiness; bliss, blissful; ecstasy; pleasure; joy, joyful; delight, delighted, delightful.

Perhaps you would like: hope, hopeful, hopefulness; faith; love; patience; paradise; euphoria; heaven; elation, elated. Or you could use: blessed, blessed be; dreams, dreamy, dreamland; enchantment, enchant, enchanting; beguile, beguiling; bewitch, bewitching; spellbinding; charm, charmed, charming; enrapture; entice, enticing; fascinate, fascinating. These suggestions can also get you started on a list of your own. Come up with more ideas.

You can also write brief quotes on rocks or break up quotes to go across several rocks. You could use this from Puck in Shakespeare's *A Midsummer Night's Dream*: "If we shadows have offended, think but this, and all is mended, That you have but slumbered here while these visions did appear." This is a great quote to include in a fairy garden, as are many more from this Shakespearean play. A little research for famous quotes on a specific topic will give you all kinds of results of different things you can work with.

Ostara Terrariums

Even if you can't do any type of outside gardening, you can create an indoor garden with a simple terrarium. Terrariums can be made out of all kinds of things. Generally people use aquariums that have had a seal leak and can no longer hold water for fish. There are tons of other ways to make terrariums though. Any type of a waterproof container, or a container that can be made to be waterproof, can serve as the terrarium base. This is another great way to reuse and upcycle items that would otherwise get thrown in the trash. Everything from an old hardcover book to a wine bottle to a light bulb (not fluorescent) can be turned into a terrarium with the proper tools.

Using old books to make a terrarium may take a lot of time, but it creates a really spectacular look. Here are the supplies you'll need to make a terrarium from a book:

- An old book (thrift stores or library book sales have them really cheap if you don't have some at home)
- Glue (for paper)
- A pencil
- A utility knife
- Plastic sheeting
- Clay (any kind of modeling clay that can be used for waterproofing)

- Potting soil, plants, small stones, or other embellishments

Your first step will be to decide whether to leave the front cover intact. If the book has beautiful endpapers, it can be nice to let the front cover lie open, but if you are short on space you may want the book to be closed. If it will stay closed, start by drawing the shape you want the hole to be on the front cover of the book. Very carefully cut it out with the utility knife. Close the book and, using that opening as your guide, trace the opening with a pencil so it appears on the first sheet of paper. Keeping the book closed (if you open the book, the holes won't line up right), use the knife and cut through several layers of the paper following the pattern. Once you remove those pages, do it several more times until you get most of the way through the book. You do not want to cut all the way down to the back cover. Keep about ¼ to ½ inch uncut to add to the base.

If you are starting with an open book, draw the shape on the top page. Then leave the book open while you cut the holes in the pages. Continue the same way as the closed book, cutting until there is a ¼ to ½ inch base.

Next, starting with the back of the book, glue the last page to the back cover, then the next page to the bottom and so on. When you get to the part that is cut out, you will continue gluing the pages together until you reach the front cover, leave that loose for now. If using an open book, leave several of the top pages loose for now.

The next step is to work on waterproofing. Take the clay and totally cover the bottom and the sides of the cavity you have created. Make sure there are no areas where water can get through and get into the pages of the book. You will need to follow the directions on the clay for letting it harden, though you obviously can't use a kiln or even an oven at too high of a temperature. After the clay has dried, add some plastic sheeting or wrapping for extra protection and glue the overlap down in between the top page and the book cover. If using an open book, glue the plastic between the last glued page and the loose ones. Then glue down any other loose pages. Gently fill the cavity with potting soil and add your plants along with any other embellishments, such as stones or moss, that you wish to include.

The plants you choose for these terrariums is important, as you will need ones that don't have giant root systems. Air plants are ideal for small terrariums. Air plants, also known as Tillandsia, do not need dirt to grow, but they do need water and plant food in order to thrive. Bonsai trees can also be planted if you have enough room and the tree is small enough.

Whatever you plant, you can also decorate these terrariums for different times of the year. An Ostara terrarium could include some of the fake colored grass used in baskets this time of year. Miniature items can often be found in craft stores for several holidays including Easter, which uses much of the same decorations and symbols as Ostara. Miniature baskets, bunnies, chicks, eggs, and even chickens are some of the items you should be able to find. If your craft store doesn't have anything small in the seasonal section, check in the dollhouse section. It's truly amazing some of the things you can find in miniature sizes these days. Pastel colored beads, glitter, sequins, or confetti can all help to make your terrarium festive. These items can all be changed out for different decorations later on. Small terrariums are a great way to add the earth element to your altar for sabbat rituals, particularly if you decorate them for the sabbat itself.

Decorate with Colors

Another great way to spruce up your surroundings is by bringing some colorful decorations into your home and/or your altar. The colors associated with Ostara are generally pastels. Pastels are associated with spring and babies—which in the animal world we see plenty of during the springtime.

Yellow is one of the most dominant colors at Ostara, and it is seen in the natural world as well. We see it in daffodils, crocuses, and tulips. It's also seen in baby chicks that start off usually yellow (some brown or black), and then when their pinfeathers come in they are a different color. By the time they are fully grown they are completely different colors from what they were when they were hatched. Yellow is also connected with the sun, which is now showing its power over the dark as the days grow longer than the night.

Orange is another color that represents the sun. Though it isn't used as often in Ostara celebrations, you can use the symbols or likeness of a big orange sun to decorate your altar. It is associated with friendship and attraction.

Green is another big color at Ostara, as the earth itself is beginning to turn green—from the grass to the buds that are starting to come out on the trees to the leaves and stems of flowers bursting through the ground. It represents fertility and abundance, and it soothes difficult situations.

Blue is for peace and tranquility. The lighter shades, such as baby blue, are associated with spring, and the Goddess in her maiden form. Blue is also another popular color of the crocus, hence one of the reasons it is associated with spring. One of the first signs spring has arrived in the north is the sighting of the bird the robin. When the robin returns, it builds its nest and lays its eggs, which are a beautiful, almost sky-blue color. Speaking of the sky, the winter in some places is often very dingy and gray with a whole lot of overcast skies. The sun doesn't get to shine down upon us too often, so when the gray clouds clear away and the sun comes out, the great big blue sky is a most welcome sight.

Violet is probably the second or third most popular color for Ostara, in a close race with pink. Violet is another color of the crocus and obviously the spring flower violets. The color violet is associated with spirituality. It complements yellow very well and is also used in its lighter shade of lavender.

Pink is highly associated with spring. Many fruit trees bloom in either pink or white, so in the spring, pink blossoms are everywhere. Pink crocuses can push their way up through snow-covered ground. The crocus is a very hearty early flower that serves a purpose—it lets people know that even if the ground is covered with snow, the earth is waking up underneath it all and pushing itself onward. Pink is also associated with love, compassion, and household peace. This color also complements yellow very well, and the two are often paired up together for decorations.

White is the color of new beginnings, like a fresh piece of paper just waiting to be written on. It is a color of innocence (the maiden), purification, and healing. Many spring flowers, including the crocus and snowdrops, and many fruit tree blossoms are white.

There are different ways to incorporate any of these colors into your decorations and altar. Of course there are candles. This time of year you can usually find candles in these colors in the shape of an egg. You can also decorate actual eggs in these colors and put them in a small basket on your altar. You can even use the plastic eggs used in egg hunts.

Ribbons are a great way to add color to your altar, and they can be used in different ways. You can tie ribbons around the base of candles or onto ritual tools. Ribbons can be draped over other decorations such as flowers or a basket. Ribbons can also be cut into lengths two to five inches long and used as confetti.

Small knickknacks of rabbits and chicks can add to your altar as well. Thrift stores are a great place to look for your decorations, as you will not only save money, you will often be able to find things that you can't find in a regular store anymore. The styles are different, and the medium / material used to make it may be different as well. Plastic is the big material used today, but at a thrift store you may be able to find wood or glass for the same, if not lower, price.

Of course any of the crafts you create can be incorporated into your altar setup as well. One of the great things about Ostara is that it is very easy for people who are not out of the closet to be able to decorate and celebrate it without people really knowing. It often falls close enough to Easter that the timing isn't too much of a giveaway. It also uses so many of the same colors and symbols that it would be hard to tell the difference between a home decorated for Ostara and one decorated for Easter—other than things such as signs that say "Happy Easter!" which will most likely be lacking in a Pagan home.

PRAYERS
AND
INVOCATIONS

…beginnings, birth, renewal, rejuvenation, balance, fertility, chang…
strength, vernal equinox, sun enters Aries, Libra in the No…
Green Man, Amalthea, Aphrodite, Blodeuwedd, Eostre, E…
…Flora, Freya, Gaia, Guinevere, Persephone, Libera, …
…npet, Umaj, Vila, Lengus MacOg, Cernunnos, Herma, The…
…Kama, Mabon Osiris, Pan, Thor, abundance, growth, health, …
…al healing, patience understanding virtue, spring, honor, content…
…hic abilities, spiritual truth, intuition, receptivity, love, inner …
…provement, spiritual awareness, purification, childhood, innocen…
…lity, creativity, communication, concentration, divination, harmo…
…abilities, prosperity, attraction, blessings, happiness, luck, mone…
…y, guidance, visions, insight, family, wishes, celebrating life cy…
…iendship, courage, attracts love, honesty, good health, emotions…
…improvement, influence, motivation, peace, rebirth, self preserv…
…minine power, freedom, optimism, new beginnings, vernal equino…
…creation, sun, apple blossom, columbine, crocus, daffodil, dais…
…sy, honeysuckle, jasmine, jonquil, lilac, narcissus, orange blosso…
…rose, rose, the fool, the magician, the priestess, justice, the st…
…ts, gathering, growth, abundance, eggs, seeds, honey, dill, aspa…

$\mathcal{W}$HEN IT COMES to the truly spiritual side of celebrating any sabbat, meditations, prayers, and invocations are what really help you connect with the Divine and your own higher self. While celebrating and feasting are a lot of fun, the real work takes place during these practices. That's not to say these things are difficult or not fun, they are however more serious and a time of deep learning as well.

If you don't already meditate, Ostara—being a time of new beginnings—is the perfect time to start. There are different forms of meditation. There are the Eastern traditions of silent meditation where you basically clear your mind, focus on your breathing, and turn your thoughts inward to whatever your body or mind needs to tell you. There is also guided meditation. While some practitioners of Eastern traditions might tell you that guided meditations are not really meditating, for those who practice guided meditations they most certainly are!

In a guided meditation, someone literally talks you through the meditation. This may be a person or a recorded track. You can read guided meditations before practicing and then try to remember the meditation as you go, but this is difficult and makes it hard to concentrate. If you have a guided meditation written out, such as those listed here, you should either enlist the help of a friend or a family member and have them read it to you when you are ready to actually practice, or you can make a recording of it as you read it yourself.

Remember this is a meditation, and you will want it to be read as such. You should lower and soften your voice, turn down your own personal volume, and reduce the speed accordingly. Read over the meditation several times silently and aloud before actually recording. You will want to make sure you leave enough time for any breaks for silent time you may need. Make sure you pay attention to pronunciation and basic grammar. Don't read it monotone or as one giant, run-on sentence. Put some time into making sure you get it right. Begin by recording just a small part. Play it back and see how it sounds to you before you record the entire meditation. Some people prefer to record on a computer and burn it to a CD or add it to an MP3 player. You can also use a small digital recorder. Whichever technology works best for you is fine.

For those new to meditating, there are a few other things you need to keep in mind.

When choosing a location to perform your meditations remember:

- Outside gives you a chance to connect with nature more, if it's not too cold. If you are too cold it will just make you miserable and distract from the meditation.

- Look for a location free of noise and other people.

- If you don't have any land, try a local park or nature preserve, just look for a spot that appears to be empty of other people.

- In the spring, a sunny location is probably fine, but in the summer you may want to move to a shaded location.

- If you are choosing a location inside, make sure it will be peaceful, quiet, and private.

- Being near a window is fine; just make sure you won't have the sun shining right into your face to distract you.

- Make your spot comfortable, whether it's a dedicated space or just temporary, make it your sanctuary using pillows, bean bags, blankets, or special meditation chairs or cushions.

- Depending on what you are comfortable with, you need to decide if you want to sit or lie down.

- You may also want to add special lighting. Candles, lava lamps, salt lamps, or colored light bulbs in blue, purple, or lavender will all add to your environment and add extra layers of peace and spirituality to your practice.

- You may want to add some meditation music to the background to help create a mood and to help relax you.

- If you are using candles, be sure to practice candle safety. Candles are good for more than just lighting, they help set a mood. Blue, white, or lavender are all spiritual colors and they can help you relax. You may also want to use colors that correspond to your meditation.

- If you have a difficult time relaxing, you may want to try a relaxing bath before meditating. Also try chamomile tea or some light stretches. Take a few moments to just sit with your eyes closed and breathe deeply in and out.

These are just a few tips and tricks that should help you get your meditation practice going. Meditation doesn't have to be difficult, in fact it's often easy, relaxing, and rather fun. Once you get used to it, your meditation time will most likely become your favorite part of the day.

Meditation for Evaluating Balance in Your Life

This meditation is pretty short, but it gives you the chance to take an inventory of what is going on in your life. Often we get so caught up in things and just go through the motions without even realizing what all is going on with us. When we take the time to sit down and basically count out all of the things going on in our lives, it can be staggering and a bit overwhelming. It can also be a wake-up call and just the motivation you need to make some changes for the better.

Begin by getting comfortable in your chosen spot and then start the meditation. If you are recording the meditation to play back aloud, or having someone read it to you, start here:

Turn off the world around you and tune in to yourself. Turn off any noises coming from anywhere else. Turn off your thoughts about the day. Turn off any distractions you may have. Feel yourself relax and unwind. Find your center and focus on being in the here and now. Nothing else matters right now. Everything else can wait. Right now is about you and your spirituality. Right now is for you.

With the equinox comes a time of balance, a time to step back and examine your life. How in balance is your life? Do you ever feel like things are out of your control? Do you feel overwhelmed, frustrated, or just plain anxious? These are all signs that something is off-kilter in your life. Something is out of whack and needs to be realigned, rebalanced. Everything has its opposite, just as the day has the night. Everything in your life has its opposite, too. The work you do has to be counteracted with play. The taking with giving. The bad times with good. If you have too much of one thing and not enough of its counterpart, you are not in balance. Even having all good times in your life throws you off. Having bad times mixed in with the good teaches you empathy and compassion. Constant good times without any bad leaves you missing out on parts of life. They may not be fun parts of life, but they are necessary. Eventually everyone will have something bad come into their life. When you aren't used to it, it can make those hard times extremely difficult to deal with. People who are used to the hard times are better equipped to deal with them simply from the practice.

Spend some time thinking about all of the things you have going on in your life. Are there equal amounts of good and bad? Work and play? Stress and peace? Or are you off balance with something? What do you do for fun? What do you do when something upsets you? How often do things upset you? Is your life pretty calm and serene, or do you find yourself jumping from crisis to crisis on an almost daily basis? *(Allow silent pause to reflect.)*

Perhaps you need help in dealing with stress. Perhaps you find yourself worrying about things you really have no control over. Maybe you take on more than you can handle and then stress out when things don't go the way you had hoped they would. Perhaps you are out of work, injured, or suffering from some sort of illness. Whatever the "bad" things are in your life, you know they are there. You need to learn to correctly identify the problem, and then find workable solutions for them. Generally, if you are too stressed out, you don't have enough fun and play in your life. This goes both ways—when you don't take the time to have fun and play, you don't get the opportunity to blow off some steam, and so you are more stressed. Always remember to fit in some good times to balance out the ones that make your life difficult.

It is important to remember that life has its ups and downs. People don't want to be sad or miserable or hurt, but it is important to remember there are lessons to be learned from the events and/or situations that lead to these feelings.

What are some of the good things going on in your life? Do you have a supportive spouse or significant other? Great friends? A good job? Do you do volunteer work to help those who are less fortunate than you? *(Allow silent pause for reflection.)*

Reminding yourself of your blessings is an excellent way to bring balance into a stressful life that often feels filled with negativity. We often forget the good and focus on the bad. When you count your blessings, you may find you do have balance in your life; the bad really does not outweigh the good. You may find it is simply where your focus lies that needs to be adjusted. *(Allow brief pause for reflection.)*

When ready, give silent thanks for the blessings in your life. Remember that when things seem bad, you can always return to focusing on your blessings in this way to achieve greater balance. Take a couple deep breaths, remind yourself of where you physically are right now, and then gently open your eyes.

Meditation for New Beginnings

In this meditation, you will focus your energies toward a successful new beginning. Whether it is a life change, a new job, a new project, or something else, this mediation will focus your energies on that new beginning and help you visualize it through to fruition.

Again you will want to record this meditation or have someone read it to you. Get into a comfortable position, close your eyes, and take several deep breaths, exhaling and inhaling for at least a count of five each time. Relax and begin your recording of the meditation here:

Ahead of you lies a new path, a new beginning. The path is cloudy and foggy and you cannot see very far down it, but you feel compelled to walk forward into the fog. With each step you take you feel you are moving closer to the fog, yet you never seem to be catching up with it. Each step you take is in clean, crisp, fog-free air. The fog remains ahead of you.

As you walk forward, you notice new things appearing on the path next to you. Images from your past show themselves to you—a childhood friend, a favorite teacher, your first girlfriend or boyfriend. As you walk past each one, they turn their gaze to follow you as you continue down the path. You are passing by your past as you move forward, but you do so with gladness. These memories bring you joy and happiness. You realize that with each new person, there was a first time you met. *(Allow a pause to recall images of the past.)*

You see yourself ride a bike for the first time, learn to swim, go to an amusement park, or go on a favorite family vacation. You see yourself getting a driver's license, graduating high school, maybe even graduating college. All are happy events from your past that you enjoy remembering. Each one of these events had a first time. Each one of these events was at one time a new beginning. Each one of these events brought you joy and happiness even though right before it happened, and maybe while it was happening, you were nervous and unsure about the situation or event. You made it through and you did so amazingly well.

With each step you take, the images at your sides become visible and clear, but the fog in front of you still remains. You continue stepping forward and the images at your sides are more recent. You are in your present now. You see people you have recently met, events that recently happened, and situations you recently found yourself in. *(Allow a brief pause)* You are happy to be reminded of these people and events and remember that they too were once a part of a new beginning. These parts of your present make you feel happy, content, and secure. You no longer worry about these things as you are now comfortable with them. You have no fear and enjoy having these aspects in your life. *(Allow a brief pause)*

As you continue walking down the road, you notice a bright light ahead of you, as if the sun is suddenly beating down upon the path. The fog begins to burn away, disappearing before your eyes. Briefly you are able to catch a glimpse of your future, of the new beginning that you are starting out in life. You can feel it pulling at you through the sun's rays. You feel comfortable in the sun's light, warm and safe, as you are able to get glimpses of your life in the future. Nothing is too clear though, as the sun quickly grows brighter and brighter until all you can see is the brightest of the sun's rays. Your future is ahead of you and it awaits in a bright, sunny, happy, and content place. You only have to keep walking forward in order to grasp it. Take some time to enjoy this feeling of anticipation. *(Allow a silent pause for reflection.)* When ready, give silent thanks for this brief glimpse and any inspiration you've gathered from it. Take a couple deep breaths, remind yourself of where you physically are right now, and gently open your eyes.

Prayer to the God and the Goddess to Bring Balance into Your Life

This prayer is designed as a way to invoke the God and the Goddess and to ask for their assistance in bringing balance into your life. When you find yourself out of balance it can take a lot of hard work to get your life back into a balance that is healthy and beneficial to you. You don't have to do this work alone, however, and can ask the divine for help. Feel free to add the name of any specific deities you work with where needed.

Dearest Lord, Father of us all, strength so bold,

be with me now as I call out to you.

Dearest Lady, Mother of us all, fairest beauty,

be with me now as I call out to you.

As the Lord and Lady balance one another out,

I, too, need balance in my life.

Often pulled too much one way, and not enough in the other,

creating instability that throws me off track.

I need to regain balance with my body, mind, and spirit,

all working together in harmony.

I ask for guidance in creating boundaries and setting limits that will encourage me to work on keeping situations and emotions in check.

I ask for guidance in showing me how I can help others when I myself am not in a time of need.

Counsel me with the steps to take,

and instruct me on what I must work on.

Help me to visualize and then realize a life lived in true balance.

Prayer to the Goddess to Assist in New Beginnings

This prayer is designed as a way to invoke the Goddess and to ask her for assistance in dealing with a new beginning you find yourself having difficulty with. New beginnings are chances to start fresh, but they may not always feel that way. Situations like a divorce can be very painful, and you may not want to be starting a new life without your spouse. Sometimes we have no choice, and new beginnings are forced upon us. Other times we are able to make the conscious decision that we start anew—those new beginnings are usually easier to cope with and to get the ball rolling. It's the changes we don't want to make that give us a hard time. This prayer is for those times. In this prayer to the Goddess, feel free to insert your own specific deity where needed.

Great Goddess, Mother to us all, giver of life and creator of all things,

life has many twists and turns and now I find myself on a new, unexpected path—

a new path I am afraid to travel alone.

I ask for your guidance, and your loving, helping hand to support me on my way.

I ask that when needed you will lead me in the right direction and steer me away from wrong turns.

Help me to keep myself on the path and to not stray away even when I am tempted.

Assist me in moving forward and not in reverse.

Comfort me when needed.

Bless my path and the journey I undertake on this path.

Encourage me in times of self-doubt.

Protect me from those willing to harm me, even if it is myself.

Embrace me in your loving arms, to give me peace and surround me in perfect love and perfect trust.

Brief Invocation for Working with the Goddess on Ostara

Maiden Goddess, soon to be Mother, known by many names,

I invoke your presence today, on this day of balance,

of equal day and equal night,

on this day of beginnings,

to join with me (us) in celebration.

Goddess of the Earth, Goddess of all Living Things, Goddess of the Spring,

join with me (us) now.

Brief Invocation for Working with the God on Ostara

Robust Lord, soon to be Father, known by many names,

I invoke your presence today, on this day of balance,

of equal day and equal night,

on this day of beginnings,

to join with me (us) in celebration.

God of the Earth, God of all living things, God of Spring,

join with me (us) now.

Offerings

There are several types of offerings to the divine that are highly acceptable this time of year. Hard-boiled eggs (peeled), milk, honey, mead, and spring flowers are the most common. For something sweet, delicious, and different, use a bowl of marshmallow fluff. If you have an outdoor altar, leave some of these offerings in the name of your deity as a thank you to them.

RITUALS
OF
CELEBRATION

beginnings, birth, renewal, rejuvenation, balance, fertility, chang
trength, vernal equinox, sun enters Aries, Libra in the Hou
Green Man, Amalthea, Aphrodite, Blodeuwedd, Eostre, E
Flora, Freya, Gaia, Guinevere, Persephone, Libera, A
pet, Umay, Vila, Aengus MacOg, Cernunnos, Herma, The
ama, Mabon Osiris, Pan, Thor, abundance, growth, health, ca
l healing, patience understanding virtue, spring, honor, contentm
hic abilities, spiritual truth, intuition, receptivity, love, inner se
rovement, spiritual awareness, purification, childhood, innocence
ty, creativity, communication, concentration, divination, harmo
bilities, prosperity, attraction, blessings, happiness, luck, money
, guidance, visions, insight, family, wishes, celebrating life cyc
ndship, courage, attracts love, honesty, good health, emotions,
improvement, influence, motivation, peace, rebirth, self preserva
nine power, freedom, optimism, new beginnings, vernal equinox
reation, sun, apple blossom, columbine, crocus, daffodil, daisy
y, honeysuckle, jasmine, jonquil, lilac, narcissus, orange blossom
rose, rose, the fool, the magician, the priestess, justice, the sta
gathering, growth, abbundance, eggs, seeds, honey, doll, as para

*R*ITUAL IS THE CEREMONIAL aspect of your practice. The time when you pull everything together and present your desires along with your honor and reverence to the deities you choose to work with in a special rite designed for a specific occasion, circumstance, or event. While ritual is often serious, it can also be lighthearted and fun, as long as it is done with respect for yourself, others, and your deities.

This section will be broken down into three different (yet similar) rituals. The first is an Ostara ritual for solitary practitioners. The second is an Ostara ritual for groups such as covens, or larger public groups, while the third Ostara ritual is written for two people.

Ostara Ritual for a Solitaire

Purpose:
To invoke the favor of the four elements and the God and the Goddess to ask them to help you restore balance in your life.

Setting:

Outside—if the weather is uncomfortable enough that it will be a distraction or in some way harm or damage the ritual or yourself, then find a location indoors to perform it.

Supplies:

Altar decorated with representations of earth, air, water, fire, the God, and the Goddess.

Pre-Ritual Preparations:

Set up your altar, being sure to include representations of the four elements—earth, air, water, and fire—along with representations of the God and Goddess. Your representations of the elements should be as close to the actual element as possible. For example, for water, use water. You can make special moon water to use in your rituals by leaving water out all night under the full moon in a clear glass container. Earth should be something such as dirt, salt, or sand. Burning incense is perfect for air. If you have issues with incense scents or the smoke, you can also waft a feather through the air. Fire should be fire—this can take the form of a candle or even a small torch. Your representations of the God and the Goddess can be statues, pictures, or even candles: silver for the Goddess, gold for the God.

Use any of the crafts you created along with some of the other ideas to decorate your altar and give it a pleasing appearance. Remember, this is where you come to honor your deities. Spend some time making their altar look nice for them as well as for yourself. Show that it really does matter to you. Be sure to also include an offering or two from those listed in the previous chapter.

The Ritual:

Begin by casting your circle. Then call in the elements as follows:

Start with the east and hold your representation of the air in your hands as you face east and say:

> *Sacred air, blessed by the Goddess*
> *and watchtowers of the east,*
> *join with me tonight,*
> *on this sacred day*
> *of equal day*
> *and equal night.*

Move to the south and hold your representation of fire in your hands and facing south, say:

Sacred fire, blessed by the Goddess
and watchtowers of the south,
join with me tonight,
on this sacred day
of equal day
and equal night.

Move to the west and hold your representation of water in your hands and facing west, say:

Sacred water, blessed by the Goddess
and watchtowers of the west,
join with me tonight,
on this sacred day
of equal day
and equal night.

Move to the north and hold your representation of the earth in your hands and facing north, say:

Sacred earth, blessed by the Goddess
and watchtowers of the north,
join with me tonight,
on this sacred day

of equal day
and equal night.

Next invite the Goddess to join you. Hold your representation of the Goddess in the air, or light a candle for her, and say:

Maiden Goddess, soon to be Mother, known by many names,
I invoke your presence today, on this day of balance,
of equal day and equal night,
on this day of beginnings,
to join with me in celebration and rejoicing of the conception
of the son, the sun child who will grow stronger each day
until his birth at Yule.
Goddess of the earth, Goddess of all living things,
Goddess of the spring,
join with me now.

Then invite the God. Hold your representation of him in the air, or light a candle for him, and say:

Robust Lord, soon to be Father, known by many names,
I invoke your presence today, on this day of balance,
of equal day and equal night,
on this day of beginnings,
to join with me in celebration and rejoicing of the conception

of the son, your son, who shall become you upon Yule,
his day of birth.
God of the earth, God of all living things, God of spring,
join with me now.

Take a moment to center yourself before continuing, then when ready, say:

Today is the day of the Vernal Equinox.
It is the day the earth awakens, with streams flowing once again.
The sap courses through trees,
bearing the announcement of new life.
Snow melts away, the grass begins its greening,
and soon flowers shall be fragrant on the breeze.
The earth has come alive once more.
Today is a day of balance and a day of new beginnings.
The light and the dark are in balance.
Today brings the dawning of a new spring.
While every ending brings a new beginning,
every new beginning will also have an end.
Today the earth begins to awaken from its slumber
and a new year of growth begins.
Today brings the dawning of a new spring,
of a new year, of a new life.
The earth sets in motion the process of growing, changing,

thriving, changing again, and eventually dying.
But for today, it brings the dawning of a new spring.
As the earth begins its cycle of new life,
so must I begin a cycle of new life.
As the earth sits in balance with the sun and the moon,
with the day and the night,
so must I sit in balance with the world, with my environment,
with my deities, and within my own self.
Each part of my life—spirit, mind, body, and soul—
must obtain balance, so that it does not outweigh any other area,
so that all have equal roles to play in my life.
As I perform this meditation, I ask for guidance and direction,
and for you to point out any areas that need my special attention in
righting them in order to achieve the balance I so desire.

At this time, perform the "Meditation for Evaluating Balance in Your Life" found in the previous chapter. Ensure that any candles that are lit will be safe while doing the meditation. When completed, take a few moments to collect your thoughts and then continue on with the following:

I know my life must have some changes made
in order for me to bring it into balance as it should be.
The areas in my life that are out of balance include:

(List what you learned is out of balance from your meditation.)

_____

_____

_____

_____

_____

_____

_____

_____

In order to restore this balance,
this spring I have new beginnings I want to make,
and I ask my Lord and Lady to guide me on my way.

Take time to think about the new beginnings you want. You may write them down if you want or just make a mental list, but make sure you remember them all, as you will need to recall them. Once you have your list ready, go ahead and continue.

The new beginnings I prepare for and commit to are:

Read or recite your list.

These changes are needed and wanted to restore
full balance to me and my life.
I ask for strength and guidance as I travel the road
laid out before me.
Changes are not always easy, but they can lead to bigger
and better circumstances,
so I will work hard to make these changes a part
of my everyday life to ensure
balance is achieved and remains a constant in my life.
New beginnings may be difficult,
but I have the strength to see it through.
The strength from the old year continues on
and enters into the new year.
I will make a practice of meditating on what the future holds for me.
I will begin that practice right now, in this time and in this space.

Perform the "New Beginnings Meditation" from the previous chapter here. When you are done, take a few moments to gather your thoughts before continuing with the following:

While my path may not always be clear,
and at times my future may seem cloudy,
I will continue down the road I know I am supposed to follow.
I will work hard to obtain and accomplish my goals,
and I will continue to set my sights higher and higher,

never backing down or giving up.
If I should slip and fall,
I will pick myself back up and continue where I left off.
I will not let setbacks get me down or dissuade me
from moving forward on my path.
I will continue to fight for what I need to
and battle my inner and outer challenges when they try
to stop me or slow me down.
I will not listen to the negativity of those around me.
I will surround myself with those who are willing to
support me and stand up for me.
I will surround myself with those who feel the same way
and who are willing to work to achieve their goals
in the same manner.
I will support those who support me.
I will help those in need and support them on their journey as well.
The springtime is the time to plant the seeds,
and these seeds I plant within me.
The springtime is the time for hope.
It is the time for desire.
It is the time for new ideas and inspiration.
I will walk hand in hand with the Lord and the Lady
to follow my path,
one on each side of me.
I will follow their guidance with grace and pleasure.

I will let go of the darkness of the past and realize that uncertainty
is not always my enemy, but may indeed be my friend.
May the coming light illuminate the path
that has been set out before me.
I will hold faith close to me and shelter it in my arms.
To the Lord and the Lady I present these offerings.

Lift offerings into the air and state what they are.

These gifts I give to honor the love and devotion I wish to express
and to thank the Lord and the Lady
for their guidance, love, and support.
I honor thee with these gifts.

Place the offerings back on the altar.

The time for changes is now, and I have made
my commitment to make them in my life.

Hold the representation of the God and say:

To my Lord, I thank you for your presence and your love.
In my devotion I bid you farewell.
Depart from me at your will.

If your representation is a candle, blow it out now.

Hold the representation of the Goddess, and say:

> *To my Lady, I thank you for your presence and your love.*
> *In my devotion I bid you farewell.*
> *Depart from me at your will.*

If your representation is a candle, blow it out now.

Turn to the east, and say:

> *Watchtower of the east,*
> *blessed air,*
> *that which keeps us all alive,*
> *depart from me at your will.*

Turn to the east, and say:

> *Watchtower of the south,*
> *blessed fire,*
> *that which brings heat to us all,*
> *depart from me at your will.*

Turn to the west, and say:

> *Watchtower of the west,*
> *blessed water,*
> *source of life,*
> *in my devotion I bid you farewell.*
> *Depart from me at your will.*

Turn to the north, and say:

> *Watchtower of the north,*
> *blessed earth,*
> *home of where all seeds grow,*
> *depart from me now at your will.*
> *The circle shall be open but unbroken.*

Ostara Ritual for a Coven or Other Large Group

This ritual is different from the previous ritual because of the simple fact there are more participants. When groups put on rituals, people do not want to stand around and listen to one or two people talk or drone on in a monotone voice. That is a sermon, not a participatory ritual, and it wouldn't do much to get people excited about the sabbat. Though this ritual will have the same themes as the solitaire's ritual and some of the same aspects, it will be presented in a different manner. A manner in which people can take on an active role instead of a passive one listening to other people do all the talking.

One of the joys of larger group rituals is you don't have to do everything yourself. Tasks for preparation, the ritual itself, and cleanup can all be delegated to different people.

Purpose:
To invoke the favor of the four elements and the God and the Goddess to ask them to help each person restore balance in their life.

Setting:
Outside—if the weather is uncomfortable enough that it will be a distraction or in some way harm or damage the ritual or yourself, then find a location indoors to perform it.

Supplies:

Three altars decorated with representations of earth, air, water, fire, the God, and the Goddess.

Pre-Ritual Preparations:

To begin, you will need three separate altars. Space them out as much as you can. If you are in a small location, you may have to have them pretty close together, but at least try to put them at different directions if possible. If you are able to hold this ritual outside, make good use of the space you have and spread them out as much as you can.

Your first altar is your elements and deities altar. It should include representations of the elements and the deities your group will be working with. The representations of the elements should be as close to the actual element as possible. For example, for water, use water. You can make special moon water to use in your rituals by leaving water out all night under the full moon in a clear glass container. Earth should be something such as dirt, salt, or sand. Burning incense is perfect for air. If people have issues with incense scents or the smoke, you can also waft a feather through the air. Fire should be fire—this can take the form of a candle or even a small torch. The representations of the God and the Goddess can be statues, pictures, or even candles: gold for the God and silver for the Goddess.

Each member of the coven should be responsible for some type of decoration. Use any of the crafts from this book along with some of the other ideas to decorate the altar and give it a pleasing appearance. This is where your group comes to honor their deities. Spend some time making the altar look nice for the deities as well as for your group. Show that it really does matter to you. Be sure to also include an offering or two from those listed in the previous chapter. This could be a job for another person as well.

Your second altar will be your altar of balance. This altar should show that everything has its opposite and this is what brings balance to the universe. For example, a picture or statuary that contains a moon and a sun or the type of scale that you put weights on one side and the item you are weighing on the other would both work. This altar should have one or two people to oversee it and to conduct the working that will take place here.

The third altar is your altar of new beginnings. This altar should include representations of the concept of new beginnings. Certain Ostara decorations lend themselves to this concept, such as eggs or baby animals like chicks and bunnies. You could also include lists of new beginnings the group members would like to make. Have members make the lists beforehand on pretty, decorative paper. Vision boards would also be a great addition and should be prepared beforehand as well. You can either give members advance warning to bring these items, or hold workshops before your ritual to actually create the items that same day. This altar should have one or two people to oversee it and to conduct the working that will take place here.

The Ritual:

When performing a group ritual, you need to have a way to purify each of the participants before they enter the sacred space. The number of people you have will dictate how you do this. For smaller groups, you can either smudge or anoint each person with a purifying oil right before they enter the sacred space. However, if you are hosting a large, public ritual it's not really realistic to smudge sixty people. Instead, you could use fireproof containers, such as cauldrons, to burn sage in on either side of the entrance. This way each participant will walk right through the smoke. In place of sage, you can also put charcoal tablets into the cauldrons and drip several drops of oil onto them as people pass through the smoke. To do this, you may have to have someone stand at each cauldron and add a few more drops each time the smoke begins to disappear.

Once everyone has entered the sacred space, you will want to cast a circle around the group. This is usually done by the high priest, high priestess, or both. If your group doesn't use a system of hierarchy, then anyone may cast the circle.

Next you will call in the elements. A different person should call in each element.

Start with the person calling in air. The person to the east should take the representation of air and hold it in his/her hands high for everyone to see, then ask everyone to face east with him/her. When he/she is ready, the person should say:

Sacred air, blessed by the Goddess
and watchtowers of the east,
join with us tonight
on this sacred day
of equal day
and equal night.

Next, the person to the south should take the representation of fire and hold it in his/her hands high for everyone to see, then ask everyone to face south with him/her. When he/she is ready, the person should say:

Sacred fire, blessed by the Goddess
and watchtowers of the south,
join with us tonight
on this sacred day
of equal day
and equal night.

Next, the person to the west should take the representation of water and hold it in his/her hands high for everyone to see, then ask everyone to face west with him/her. When he/she is ready, the person should say:

> *Sacred water, blessed by the Goddess*
> *and watchtowers of the west,*
> *join with us tonight*
> *on this sacred day*
> *of equal day*
> *and equal night.*

Next, the person to the north should take the representation of earth and hold it in his/her hands high for everyone to see, then ask everyone to face north with him/her. When he/she is ready, the person should say:

> *Sacred earth, blessed by the Goddess*
> *and watchtowers of the north,*
> *join with us tonight*
> *on this sacred day*
> *of equal day*
> *and equal night.*

Next, invite the Goddess to join your group. This is also usually done by a high priestess or high priest, but it doesn't have to be. This person should hold the representation of the Goddess in the air, or light a candle for her, and say:

Maiden Goddess, soon to be Mother, known by many names,
we invoke your presence today, on this day of balance,
of equal day and equal night,
on this day of beginnings,
to join with us in celebration and rejoicing of the conception
of the son, the sun child who will grow stronger
each day until his birth at Yule.
Goddess of the earth, Goddess of all living things,
Goddess of the spring,
join with us now.

Last invite the God. Again often done by the high priest or high priestess, but whoever does so should hold the representation of the God in the air, or light a candle for him, and say:

Robust Lord, soon to be Father, known by many names,
we invoke your presence today, on this day of balance,
of equal day and equal night,
on this day of beginnings,
to join with us in celebration and rejoicing of the conception

of the son, your son, who shall become you upon Yule,
his day of birth.
God of the earth, God of all living things, God of spring,
join with us now.

If you have a high priest or high priestess, one of them should take over right now, otherwise, someone else can take the lead for this part. This person should be sure to walk around and be animated while saying the following:

Today is the day of the Vernal Equinox.
It is the day the earth awakens, with streams flowing once again.
The sap courses through trees,
bearing the announcement of new life.
Snow melts away, the grass begins its greening,
and soon flowers shall be fragrant on the breeze.
The earth has come alive once more.
Today is a day of balance and a day of new beginnings.
The light and the dark are in balance.
Today brings the dawning of a new spring.
As the earth begins its cycle of new life,
so must we begin a cycle of new life as well.
As the earth sits in balance with the sun and the moon,
with the day and the night,

so must we sit in balance with the world, with our environment,
with our deities, and within our own selves.

At this point, the person(s) who are overseeing the balance altar should take over and say:

Each part of our lives—spirit, mind, body, and soul—
must obtain balance, so that one does not outweigh any other area,
so that all have equal roles to play in our lives.
Take time now to come forward to this altar
and gaze upon the symbols of balance.
Meditate briefly on what is out of balance in your life.

The overseers should continue inviting people to step forward to the altar. As they come forward, the overseers ask them questions such as "What is out of balance in your life?" or "What areas of your life are taking over and what areas are you lacking in?" The number of people you are working with will dictate how long this will take. Most people will only remain a few minutes and several people will be able to gather around the altar at one time.

Once everyone has had a chance to approach the altar, the overseer should close the altar down with:

Some changes must be made in order for us to bring our lives into
balance as it should be.
In order to restore this balance,
this spring we have new beginnings we want to make,
and we ask our Lord and Lady to guide us on our way.

At this time, those overseeing the new beginnings altar should take over and say:

New beginnings are needed to make necessary changes in our lives.
Take time now to come forward to this altar
and gaze upon the symbols of new beginnings.
Meditate briefly on what new beginnings you need in your life.

The overseers should continue inviting people to come forward to the altar and ask questions such as "What new beginnings do you have planned?" and "What changes do you want to make in your life?" After everyone has had a chance to come forward to the altar, it should be closed down by saying:

These changes brought forward in the minds of our people today
are needed and wanted to restore full balance to our lives.
We ask for strength and guidance as we travel the road
laid out before us.

Changes are not always easy, but can lead to bigger
and better circumstances,
so we will work hard to make these changes a part
of our everyday lives to ensure
balance is achieved and remains a constant in our lives

The ritual leader should again take control and say:

New beginnings may be difficult,
but we have the strength to see it through.
The strength from the old year continues on,
and enters into the new year.
While our path may not always be clear,
and at times our my future may seem cloudy,
we will continue down the road we know we are supposed to follow.
We will work hard to obtain and accomplish our goals
and always continue to set our sights higher and higher,
never backing down or giving up.
The springtime is the time to plant the seeds,
and these seeds we plant within ourselves.
The springtime is the time for hope.
It is the time for desire.
It is the time for new ideas and inspiration.

We will walk hand in hand with the Lord and the Lady
to follow our paths,
and we will follow their guidance with grace and pleasure.
To the Lord and the Lady we present these offerings.

Lift offerings into the air and state what they are.

These gifts we give to honor the love and devotion we wish to express
and to thank the Lord and the Lady
for their guidance, love, and support.
We honor thee with these gifts.

Place the offerings back on the altar.

The time for changes is now, and we have made our
commitments to make them in our life.

The leader will hold the representation of the God and say:

To our Lord, we thank you for your presence and your love.
In our devotion we bid you farewell.
Depart from us at your will.

If the representation is a candle, it can now be blown out.

The leader will hold the representation of the Goddess and say:

To our Lady, we thank you for your presence and your love.
In our devotion we bid you farewell.
Depart from us at your will.

If the representation is a candle, it can be blown out now.

The person at the east should instruct everyone to face east as he or she says:

Watchtower of the east,
blessed air,
that which keeps us all alive,
depart from us at your will.

The person at the south should instruct everyone to face the south as he or she says:

Watchtower of the south,
blessed fire,
that which brings heat to us all,
depart from us at your will.

The person at the west should instruct everyone to face the west as he or she says:

Watchtower of the west,
blessed water,
source of life,
in our devotion we bid you farewell.
Depart from us at your will.

The person at the north should instruct everyone to face the north as he or she says:

Watchtower of the north,
blessed earth,
home of where all seeds grow,
depart from us at your will.

Everyone performing the ritual should end with:

The circle shall be open but unbroken.

Ostara Ritual for Two People

This ritual is designed for just two people to complete. These can be any two people, it does not have to be a male and a female. This ritual may be performed by spouses, friends, siblings, even a parent with a child.

Because this ritual has a lot to do with balance, you will be sharing the responsibilities for performing the actual ritual. You should also share in the preparation of the ritual. For this ritual, you will set up your altar just the same as if you were performing it as a solitaire.

Purpose:

To invoke the favor of the four elements and the God and the Goddess to ask them to help each person restore balance in their life.

Setting:

Outside—if the weather is uncomfortable enough that it will be a distraction or in some way harm or damage the ritual or yourself, then find a location indoors to perform it.

Supplies:

An altar decorated with representations of earth, air, water, fire, the God, and the Goddess.

Pre-Ritual Preparations:

Set up the altar being sure to include representations of the four elements—earth, air, water, and fire—along with representations of the God and the Goddess. The representations of the elements should be as close to the actual element as possible. For example, for water, use water. Special moon water can be made to use in your rituals by leaving water out all night under the full moon in a clear glass container. Earth should be something such as dirt, salt, or sand. Burning incense is perfect for air. If anyone has issues with incense scents or the smoke, you can also waft a feather through the air. Fire should be fire—this can take the form of a candle or even a small torch. The representations of the God and the Goddess can be statues, pictures, or even candles: gold for the God and silver for the Goddess.

Use any of the crafts you created along with some of the other ideas to decorate your altar and give it a pleasing appearance. Each participate should make at least one decoration for the altar. Remember this is where you come to honor your deities. Spend some time making their altar looks nice for them as well as yourself. Show that it really does matter to you. Be sure to also include an offering or two from those listed in the previous chapter.

The Ritual:

Begin by casting your circle. Then, call in the elements as follows:

Start with your representation of air. One person should hold it in his/her hands and as you are both facing east say:

> *Sacred air, blessed by the Goddess*
> *and watchtowers of the east,*
> *join with us tonight*
> *on this sacred day*
> *of equal day*
> *and equal night.*

The second person should move to the south and hold the representation of fire in his or her hands and as you both face south say:

> *Sacred fire, blessed by the Goddess*
> *and watchtowers of the south,*
> *join with us tonight*
> *on this sacred day*
> *of equal day*
> *and equal night.*

The first person should now move to the west and hold the representation of water in his or her hands and as you both face west say:

> *Sacred water, blessed by the Goddess*
> *and watchtowers of the west,*
> *join with us tonight*
> *on this sacred day*
> *of equal day*
> *and equal night.*

The other person should go to the north and hold the representation of the earth in his or her hands as you both face north and say:

> *Sacred earth, blessed by the Goddess*
> *and watchtowers of the north,*
> *join with us tonight*
> *on this sacred day*
> *of equal day*
> *and equal night.*

Next invite the Goddess to join you, if one person is female, she should hold the representation of the Goddess in the air or light a candle for her, and say:

> *Maiden Goddess, soon to be Mother, known by many names,*
> *we invoke your presence today, on this day of balance,*
> *of equal day and equal night,*
> *on this day of beginnings,*
> *to join with us in celebration.*
> *Goddess of the earth, Goddess of all living things,*
> *Goddess of the spring,*
> *join with us now.*

Then invite the God. If one of the participants is a male, he should hold the representation of the God in the air or light a candle for him, and say:

> *Robust Lord, soon to be Father, known by many names,*
> *we invoke your presence today, on this day of balance,*
> *of equal day and equal night,*
> *on this day of beginnings,*
> *to join with us in celebration.*
> *God of the earth, God of all living things, God of spring,*
> *join with me now.*

Whoever spoke last should allow the other to speak next. Take turns through these next lines to keep the balance between the two of you:

> *Today is the day of the Vernal Equinox.*
> *It is the day the earth awakens, with streams flowing once again.*
> *The sap courses through trees, bearing the announcement*
> *of new life.*
> *Snow melts away, the grass begins its greening,*
> *and soon flowers shall be fragrant on the breeze.*
> *The earth has come alive once more.*
> *Today is a day of balance and a day of new beginnings.*
> *Today brings the dawning of a new spring.*
> *The light and the dark are in balance.*
> *All existence comes together in balance.*

At this point the two of you should turn and face each other, holding both hands.

Using the list on the next page as a starting point, you will take turns stating a concept. The other person will respond with its opposite or its counterpart and then give the next concept on the list. The first person will respond with that concept's opposite and go on to the next word. This will continue back and forth. Each time you come up with a word or concept, your partner will balance it out with the opposite. When you get through the list, come up with more words on your own, and see how many pairs you can come up with.

dark	yin	day	active
peace	love	wet	noon
slow	white	lost	male
here	life	protect	stop
left	up	end	over
perfect	friend	thick	pain
soft	easy	last	open

These will give you a jumping point to move on to other concepts. Feel free to jump around or simply use ones that you come up with instead. When you can't think of any more, you may release hands on move on with the ritual.

At this time, you may perform the "Meditation for Evaluating Balance in Your Life" from the previous chapter. When you are done, you will take turns as you continue on. The first person will pose the following question to the other who will then answer it (either out loud or silently to him/herself) and then will ask the same question of the first person. Take your time thinking about your answers and actually answering the question. Do not feel rushed and do not rush the other person. You may even want to sit during this time to allow for a more meditative state of mind while giving these questions some deep thought. If you are comfortable enough with the other person, you may want to sit while facing each other and holding hands. The first person will say:

On this day of balance, take a moment to think—
a moment to reflect on your life.
Is your life in balance, and if not, what do you need to change in
order to make it so?

The second person should answer. You will know when the other person is finished if they are answering silently as they will then repeat the question for you to answer. When the first person is done answering the first question, they may move on to this next one.

Spring is the time of new beginnings, of new life.
As the flowers burst through the ground,
and the buds burst into leaves and flowers,
new life surrounds us all.
What do you need to plant to bring new growth into your life?

This question is done the same as the previous one, the second person may answer out loud or silently and when finished answering, ask the first person the same question. When the first person is done answering, he/she will move the ritual on.

At this time you will each again take turns with the first person starting.

We have brought forth our desires, our needs,
to bring balance and new growth into our lives.
Whether that growth be spiritual, emotional, mental, or physical,
we ask for the blessings of our lord and lady.
We ask for strength and courage when needed.
We ask for empathy and compassion when needed.
Help us to see the path set before us.
Help to light our way.

Say the following together:

To the Lord and the Lady we present these offerings.

Lift offerings into the air and state what they are.

These gifts we give to honor the love and devotion we wish
to express and to thank the Lord and the Lady
for their guidance, love, and support.
We honor thee with these gifts.

Place the offerings back on the altar.

Begin to close your ritual down. If a male is present, he should hold the representation of the God and say:

To my Lord, we thank you for your presence and your love.

In our devotion we bid you farewell.
Depart from us at your will.

If the representation is a candle, blow it out now.

If a female is present she should hold the representation of the Goddess and say:

To my Lady, we thank you for your presence and your love.
In our devotion we bid you farewell.
Depart from us at your will.

If the representation is a candle, blow it out now.

Both turn and face west while one says:

Watchtower of the west,
blessed water,
source of life,
in our devotion we bid you farewell.
Depart from us at your will.

Both turn and face north while the other one says:

Watchtower of the north,
blessed earth,

home of where all seeds grow,
depart from us at your will.

Both turn and face the east with the first one saying:

Watchtower of the east,
blessed air,
that which keeps us all alive,
depart from us at your will.

Both turn to face the south and the second person says:

Watchtower of the south,
blessed fire,
that which brings heat to us all,
depart from us at your will.

Both say together:

The circle shall be open but remain unbroken.

CORRESPONDENCES
FOR
OSTARA

beginnings, birth, renewal, rejuvenation, balance, fertility, chang

strength, vernal equinox, sun enters Aries, Libra in the Sou

Green Man, Amalthea, Aphrodite, Blodeuwedd, Eostre, Eo

Flora, Freya, Gaia, Guinevere, Persephone, Libera, A

pet, Umaj, Vila, Aengus Mac Og, Cernunnos, Herma, The

ema, Mabon Osiris, Pan, Thor, abundance, growth, health, ca

l healing, patience understanding virtue, spring, honor, contentm

hic abilities, spiritual truth, intuition, receptivity, love, inner se

provement, spiritual awareness, purification, childhood, innocence

ty, creativity, communication, concentration, divination, harmo

bilities, prosperity, attraction, blessings, happiness, luck, money

, guidance, visions, insight, family, wishes, celebrating life cyc

endship, courage, attracts love, honesty, good health, emotions,

improvement, influence, motivation, peace, rebirth, self preserva

inine power, freedom, optimism, new beginnings, vernal equinox

reation, sun, apple blossom, columbine, crocus, daffodil, daisy

y, honeysuckle, jasmine, jonquil, lilac, narcissus, orange blossom

rose, rose, the fool, the magician, the priestess, justice, the st

athering, growth, abundance, eggs, seeds, honey, dill, aspa

Spiritual Focus and Key Words
Balance
birth
change
fertility
growing in strength
light
new beginnings
rebirth
rejuvenation
renewal

Magickal Focus
Abundance
balance
change
fertility
growth

lust

new beginnings

new love

passion

prosperity

purification

Suggested Workings

Bonfires

creating outdoor sacred spaces and altars

divinations focused on the coming year and bringing balance
to one's life

planning and creating fairy, flower, and vegetable gardens

purifying and protecting the home and all who live there
including animals

Astrological Timing and Associated Planets

The Vernal Equinox marks when the sun hits its zenith, the point on the celestial sphere directly over the equator. Sun enters the sign of Aries in the Northern Hemisphere and Libra in the Southern Hemisphere.

Archetypes

FEMALE

Goddess of fertility

Mother of the Earth

the Goddess in the form of the Maiden

MALE

God in the form of a young, lustful man who will soon become
the father

God of the wild

the Green Man

Deities and Heroes

GODDESSES

Amalthea (Greek)

Aphrodite / Venus (Greco-Roman)

Blodewedd (Welsh)

Eos (Greek)

Eostre (Germanic)

Epona (Celtic)

Flora (Roman)

Freya (Norse)

Gaia (Greek)

Guinevere (Welsh/Arthurian)

Libera (Roman)

Maia (Greek)

Persephone (Greek)

Rati (Hindu)

Renpet (Egyptian)

Umaj (Russian)

Vila (Slavic)

Gods

Aengus MacOg (Irish),

Cernunnos/Herne (Anglo-Celtic)

the Dagda (Irish)

Eros/Cupid (Greco-Roman)

the Green Man (European/North American)

Kama (Hindu)

Mabon (Anglo-Welsh)

Osiris (Egyptian)

Pan (Greek)

Thor (Norse)

Colors

Green: Abundance, calming, fertility, growth, health, new
     beginnings, prosperity

Light blue: Calmness, patience, tranquility, understanding

Pink: Affection, contentment, harmony, honor, love, spiritual
  healing, spring, tenderness, virtue
Silver: The Goddess, intuition, the inner self, night, psychic
  abilities, receptivity, spiritual truth
Violet: Healing, intuition, self-improvement, spiritual awareness
White: Childhood, cleansing, divination, healing, innocence,
  peace, protection, purification, truth
Yellow: Attraction, creativity, communication, joy, planning,
  psychic ability, the sun, vitality

Herbs

Broom: Calming, communication, concentration, divination,
  harmony, intuition, prosperity, purification
High John Root: Attraction, blessings, divination, happiness,
  love, luck, peace, prosperity, psychic abilities, strength,
  support, well-being
Irish Moss: Luck, money
Lemon Grass: Psychic awareness, purification

Trees

Alder: Clarity, divination, guidance, intuition, rebirth,
  renewal, transformation, truth, visions
Apple: Attraction, beauty, beginnings, blessings, divination,
  fertility, innocence, insight, love, renewal, relationships,
  strength, well-being

Hawthorn: Creativity, family, fertility, happiness, love, luck, peace, prosperity, purity, relationships, self-work, wishes

Flowers

Apple Blossom: Celebrating life cycles, friendship, love, peace

Columbine: Courage

Crocus: Attracts love

Daffodil: Fertility, honors the gods and goddesses of spring, love, wishing

Daisy: Attracts love and lust

Honeysuckle: Honesty, psychic awareness, prosperity

Jasmine: Dreams, love, peace, sex, spirituality

Jonquil: Affection, love

Lilac: Beauty, love, protection, purification, reveals past lives

Narcissus: Harmony, love, peace

Orange Blossom: Beauty, love, marriage

Primrose: Attracts spring faeries and love

Rose: Beauty, love, luck, peace, protection, psychic powers, sex

Tulip: Dreams, happiness, love, purification

Violets: Healing, love, luck, lust, peace, sleep, spiritual healing, wishes

Crystals and Stones

Agate: Courage, love, protection, strength

Aquamarine: Courage, peace, psychic awareness, purification, self-expression

Bloodstone: Courage, self-confidence, strength

Metals

Silver: Ambition, attraction, beginnings, calm, creativity, emotions, energy, improvement, influence, intuition, love, luck, lust, motivation, peace, prosperity, psychic abilities, purification

Animals, Totems, and Mythical Creatures

Bees: Symbolize new life and good health, produce honey —a gift from the Gods

Boar: A symbol of masculine power. Meat from the boar was served to the deities. Consuming the boar's meat gave one strength.

Butterflies: Symbolize rebirth as they emerge from their cocoons as a different creature

Chicks: Represent the birth of a new generation, fertility, and things to come

Hedgehog: Symbolizes self-preservation

Horse: Symbolizes feminine power and freedom, the return of the Goddess from the underworld bringing the spring

Phoenix: A mythical creature of optimism that symbolizes rebirth and new beginnings

Pooka: Magickal Irish creature said to be half man and half rabbit (or other animal), symbolizes fertility and was a servant who helped bring the power of the Vernal Equinox to the land, woods, and field

Rabbit: A symbol of fertility, as rabbits multiply quickly and in large numbers, symbol of prosperity and abundance

Ram: Symbolizes young masculine power, particularly of a lustful nature, and the power to procreate. It is also the symbol of Aries

Robin: The first sign of spring. Shows it is the end of the cold winter, and announces the coming of the sun and warmer days

Scents for Oils, Incense, Potpourri, or Just Floating in the Air

Apple blossom

clean crisp air

columbine

crocus

daffodil

daisy

honey

honeysuckle

jasmine

jonquil

lilac

narcissus

orange blossom

primrose

rose

any spring floral scent

rain

Tarot Keys

The Empress

the Fool

the Magickian

the Priestess

Strength

Justice

the Star

Symbols and Tools

Baskets: Gathering and encouraging growth and abundance

Eggs: Creation and fertility

Hare: Symbol of the holiday and the Goddess Eostre

Seeds: Fertility, new beginnings, and new goals

Foods

Asparagus

dill

eggs

honey

lamb

lettuce

radishes

seafood

spring onions

Drinks

Drinks that come in spring colors

mead

Activities and Traditions of Practice

Blessing seeds

cascarones

coloring eggs

egg hunts

home blessings

making plans for the year

painting or carving runes to represent new ideas or qualities
   you want to bring into your life

preparing a garden

spring cleaning

start seedlings

starting garden plants indoors

Acts of Service

Assisting with the homeless, as most temporary shelters will
soon be closing

litter pick-up (as the snows melt the garbage is unburied!)

doing community gardening or community farming

Alternate Names for Ostara
in other Pagan Traditions

Alban Eiler (Celtic, meaning the Light of the Earth)

Festival of Summer Finding (Asatru)

Vernal or Spring Equinox

Holidays or Traditions Occurring During
Ostara in the Northern Hemisphere

RELIGIOUS

Dionysus or Bacchus Day (Greco Roman, March 16–17)

Annunciation of the Blessed Virgin Mary or Lady Day
(Catholic, March 25)

Palm Sunday (Christian, the Sunday before Easter)

Good Friday (Christianity, the Friday before Easter)

Easter (Christian, the first Sunday after the first full moon
after the Spring Equinox)

Passover (Jewish, fifteenth day of Nisan, which begins on the night of the full moon after the northern Vernal Equinox)

SECULAR

St. Patrick's Day (while originally the Catholic Feast Day of a Saint, it is celebrated more as a secular holiday in the United States on March 17)

Holidays or Traditions Occurring During Ostara in the Southern Hemisphere

RELIGIOUS

Feast of Jupiter, Juno, Minerva (Nova Roma)

Michaelmas (Catholic Christians)

Birth of the Virgin Mary (Catholic Christian, September 8)

SECULAR

Floriade (largest flower festival in the Southern Hemisphere)

FURTHER
READING

Books

Banks, Mary Macleod. *British Calendar Customs: Scotland*, THREE VOLUMES: vols. 1, 2 & 3. London: Folklore Society, 1937.

Dugan, Ellen. *Seasons of Witchery: Celebrating the Sabbats with the Garden Witch*. Woodbury, MN: Llewellyn Publications, 2012.

Emerson, Lisa. *Ostara for the Youngest Witchlings*. Seattle, WA: Amazon Digital Services, 2013.

Kyrja. *Rupert's Tales: The Wheel of the Year—Samhain, Yule, Imbolc, and Ostara*. Atglen, PA: Schiffer Publishing, 2012.

Lee, Jodi. *Ostara: Creating New Pagan Family Traditions*. Seattle, WA: Amazon Digital Services, 2012.

Nar. *Recipes for Ostara*. Seattle, WA: CreateSpace Independent Publishing Platform, 2012.

Jackson, Ellen. *The Spring Equinox: Celebrating the Greening of the Earth*. Minneapolis, MN: Millbrook Press, 2012.

Online

The Mysterious Megaliths of New England:
http://planetvermont.com/pvq/v9n1/megaliths.html

Aphrodite: Greek Goddess of Love & Beauty:
http://www.theoi.com/Olympios/Aphrodite.html

Floromancy—Divination with Flowers—The Druid's Egg:
Imbolc–Ostara 2009: http://www.youtube.com
/watch?v=e3IFVQhTqq4

Mythology Guide: http://www.online-mythology.com/clytie/

Religious Tolerance: http://www.religioustolerance.org
/spequi2.htm#

The Sacred Fire—Celtic Festivals:
http://www.sacredfire.net/festivals.html

Venus—Roman Goddess of Love and Beauty:
http://www.goddess.ws/venus.html

BIBLIOGRAPHY

Books

Breathnach, Sarah Ban. *Mrs. Sharp's Traditions: Reviving Victorian Family Celebrations of Comfort and Joy.* New York: Scribner, 2001.

Buckland, Raymond. *The Fortune-Telling Book: The Encyclopedia of Divination and Soothsaying.* Canton, MI: Visible Ink Press, 2003.

Connor, Kerri. *The Pocket Spell Creator: Magickal References at Your Fingertips.* Pompton Plains, NJ: New Page Books, 2003.

Goudsward, David, with Robert E. Stone. *America's Stonehenge: The Mystery Hill Story.* Boston, MA: Branden Books, 2003.

Hutton, Ronald. *Stations of the Sun: A History of the Ritual Year in Britain.* New York: Oxford University Press, 1996.

Jordan, Michael. *Dictionary of the Gods and Goddesses.* New York: Facts on File, 2005.

Kimmel, Eric. *The Birds' Gift: A Ukrainian Easter Story.* New York: Holiday House, 1999.

Kynes, Sandra. *Llewellyn's Complete Book of Correspondences: A Comprehensive and Cross-Referenced Resource for Pagans & Wiccans.* Woodbury, MN: Llewellyn Publications, 2013.

McCoy, Edain. *Ostara: Customs, Spells & Rituals for the Rites of Spring.* St. Paul, MN: Llewellyn Publications, 2003.

O'Gaea, Ashleen. *Celebrating the Seasons of Life: Samhain to Ostara, Lore Rituals, Activities, and Symbols.* Pompton Plains, NJ: New Page Books, 2004.

Shaw, Phillip. *Pagan Goddesses in the Early Germanic World: Eostre, Hreda and the Cult of Matrons.* London: Bristol Classical Press, 2011.

Trotter, James M. *Reading Hosea in Achaemenid Yehud.* London: Continuum International Publishing Group, 2001.

Online

Angel, Paul Tudor. "The Mysterious Megaliths of New England," *Planet Vermont*. Accessed February 20, 2014, http://planetvermont.com/pvq/v9n1/megaliths.html.

Bott, Adrian. "Hunting the spurious Eostre Hare," *Cavalorn LiveJournal Blog*, March 13, 2013. Accessed February 17, 2014, http://cavalorn.livejournal.com/585924.html.

"Celtic Druid's Spring Equinox," Ireland's Druidschool. Accessed August 3, 2014, http://www.druidschool.com/site/1030100/page/765341.

"Celtic Festivals," The Sacred Fire. Accessed February 20, 2014, http://www.sacredfire.net/festivals.html.

Dickman, Jean-Andrew. "The Coming of Eostre," *Cricket*; March 2002, Vol. 29 Issue 7, p. 16. Accessed February 17, 2014, http://connection.ebscohost.com/c/short-stories/6190686/coming-eostre.

"Fernacre Stone Circle," Cornwall's Archeological Heritage: A field guide to accessible sites. Accessed February 20, 2014, http://www.historic-cornwall.org.uk/a2m/bronze_age/stone_circle/fernacre/fernacre.htm.

Gill, N. S. "Bacchanalia," Ancient History—About.com. Accessed February 10, 2014, http://ancienthistory.about.com/od/dionysusmyth/g/Bacchanalia.htm.

"International Day of Nowruz," The United Nations. Accessed February 20, 2014, http://www.un.org/en/events/nowruzday/.

Lady Hectate. "Sabbat Celebrations." Hecate's Cauldron. Accessed February 18, 2014, http://www.hecatescauldron.org/sabbats.htm.

Lindemans, Micha F. "Venus," Encyclopedia Mythica. Edited May 26, 1999, accessed August 3, 2014, http://www.pantheon.org/articles/v/venus.html.

"Loughcrew Passage Tombs," Megalithic Ireland. Accessed February 20, 2014, http://www.megalithicireland.com/loughcrew.htm.

"Mnajdra Temples," Heritage Malta. Accessed May 14, 2014, http://heritagemalta.org/museums-sites/mnajdra-temples/.

"Pyramid of Kukulkan at Chich'en Itza," Atlas Obscura. Accessed February 20, 2014, http://www.atlasobscura.com/places/pyramid-kukulcan-chichen-itza.

Sofaer, Anna P., and Sinclair, Rolf M. "Astronomical Markings at Three Sites on Fajada Butte," from *Astronomy and Ceremony in the Prehistoric Southwest*, John B. Carlson and W. James Judge, editors, Maxwell Museum of Anthropology, Anthropological Papers, No. 2, 1983, as posted on *Solstice Project*. Accessed on February 20, 2014, http://www.solsticeproject.org/astromark.htm.

Van De Bogart, Willard. "Stones in the Sky—Part III: First section: The Secrets of Angkor Wat–Cambodian Expedition II," Earth Portals. Accessed February 20, 2014, http://www.earthportals.com/Portal_Messenger /stonesinsky3.html.

White, René. "New Equinox Features Discovered at Clarke County Solstice Site," *Clarke Daily News*, September 21, 2012. Accessed February 20, 2014, http://www.clarkedailynews.com/new-equinox-features -discovered-at-clarke-county-solstice-site/.

INDEX

R

S

About the Author

Kerri Connor (Chicagoland, IL) is the High Priestess of The Gathering Grove and has been practicing her craft for twenty-five years. She is the author of three other books of magic, and her writing has appeared in *The Blessed Bee, Sage Woman, PanGaia,* and *newWitch*. She runs The Pagan Review, a website that provides reviews of Pagan products. She also recently started Nurturing Necessities, a non-profit charitable organization.

Other Books by Kerri Connor

Spells for Tough Times:
Crafting Hope When Faced with Life's Thorniest Challenges